This book belongs to

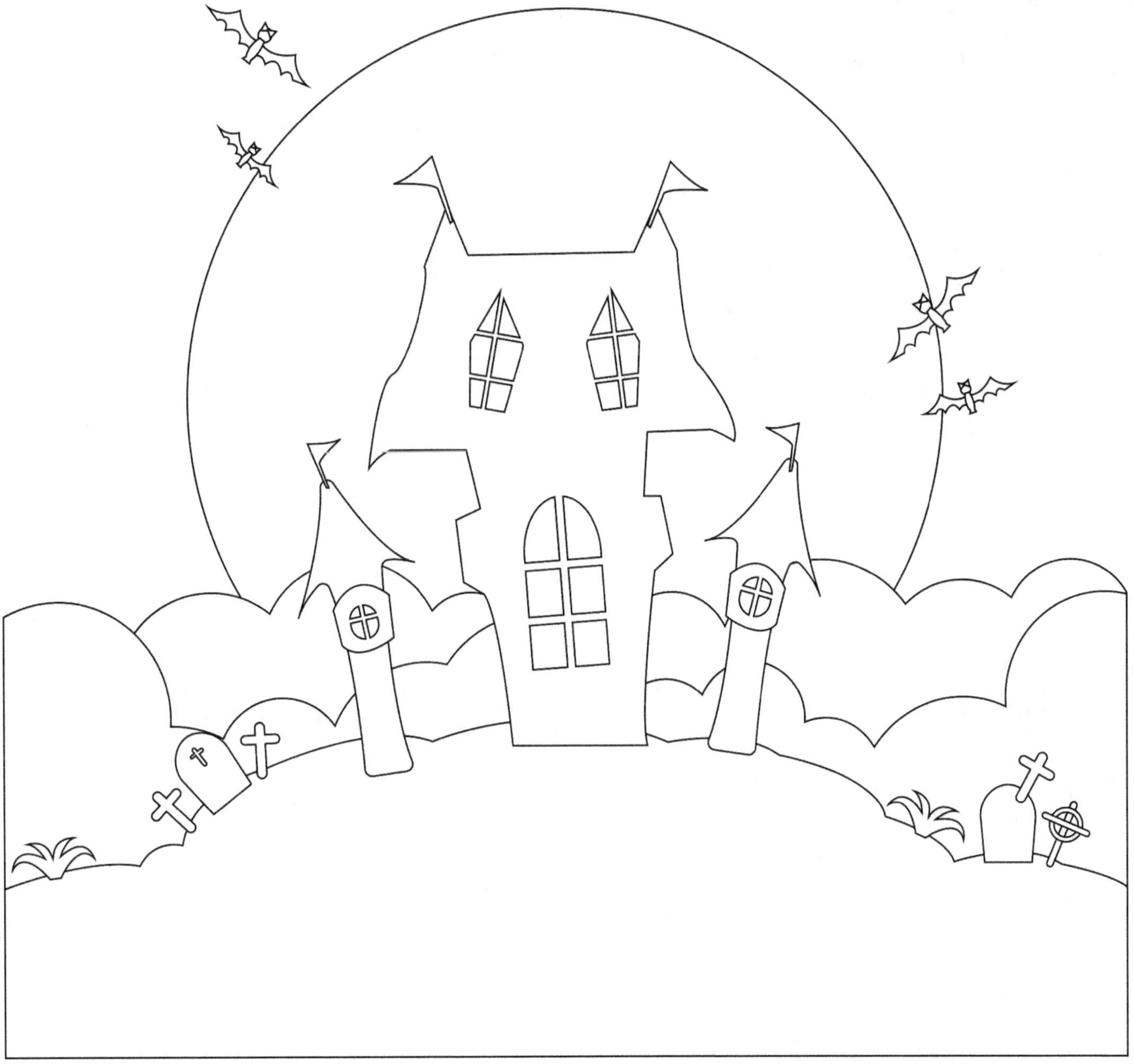

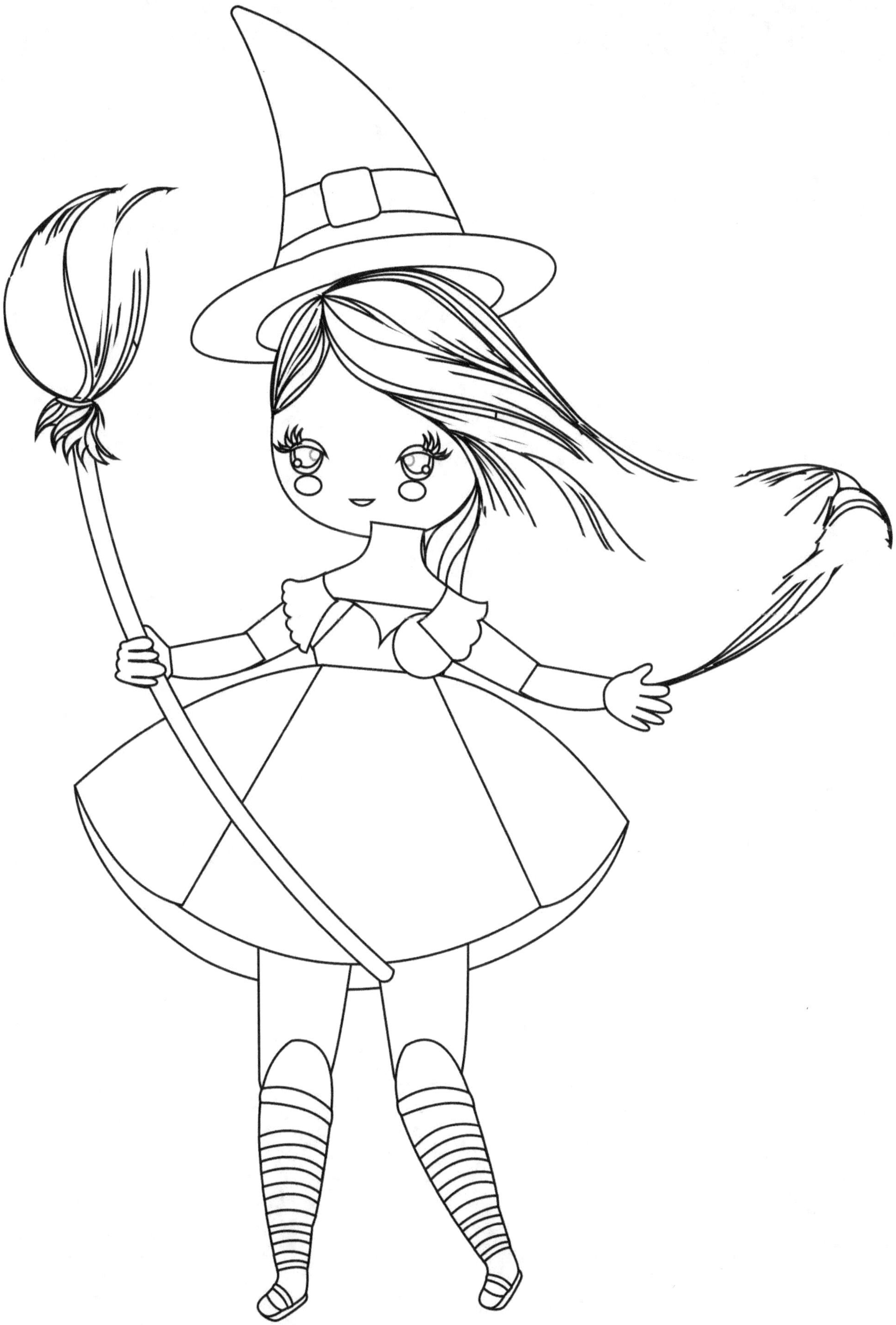

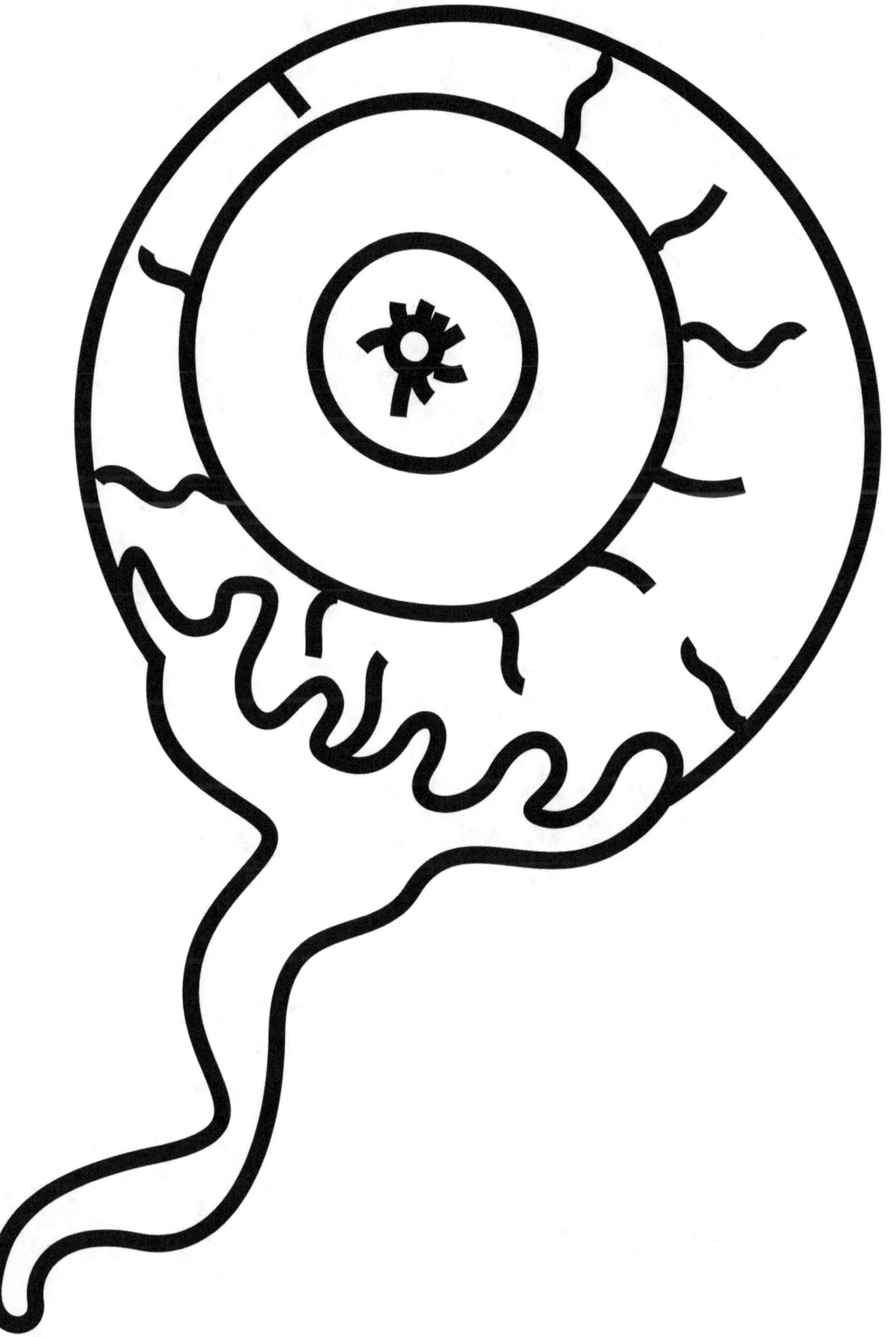

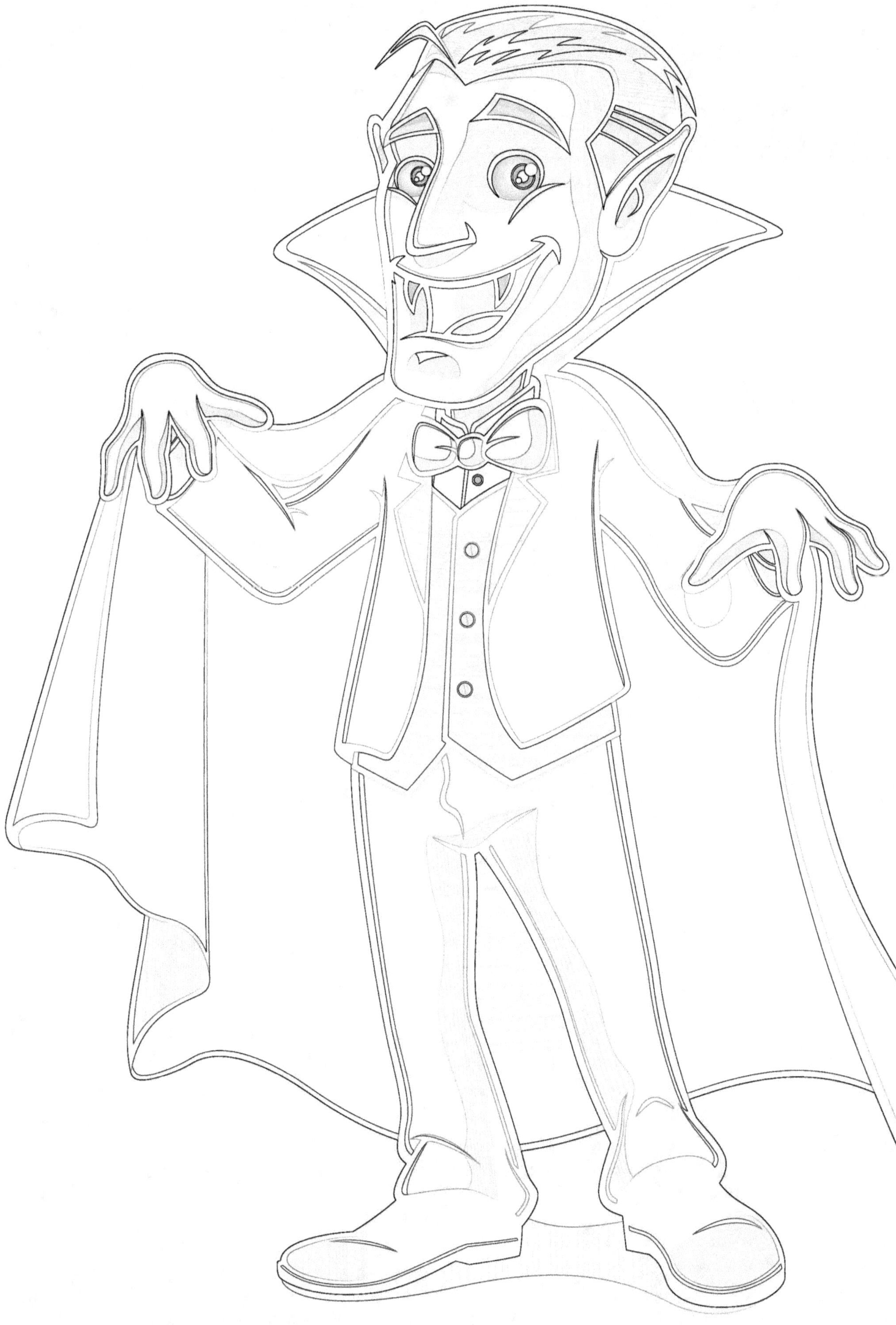

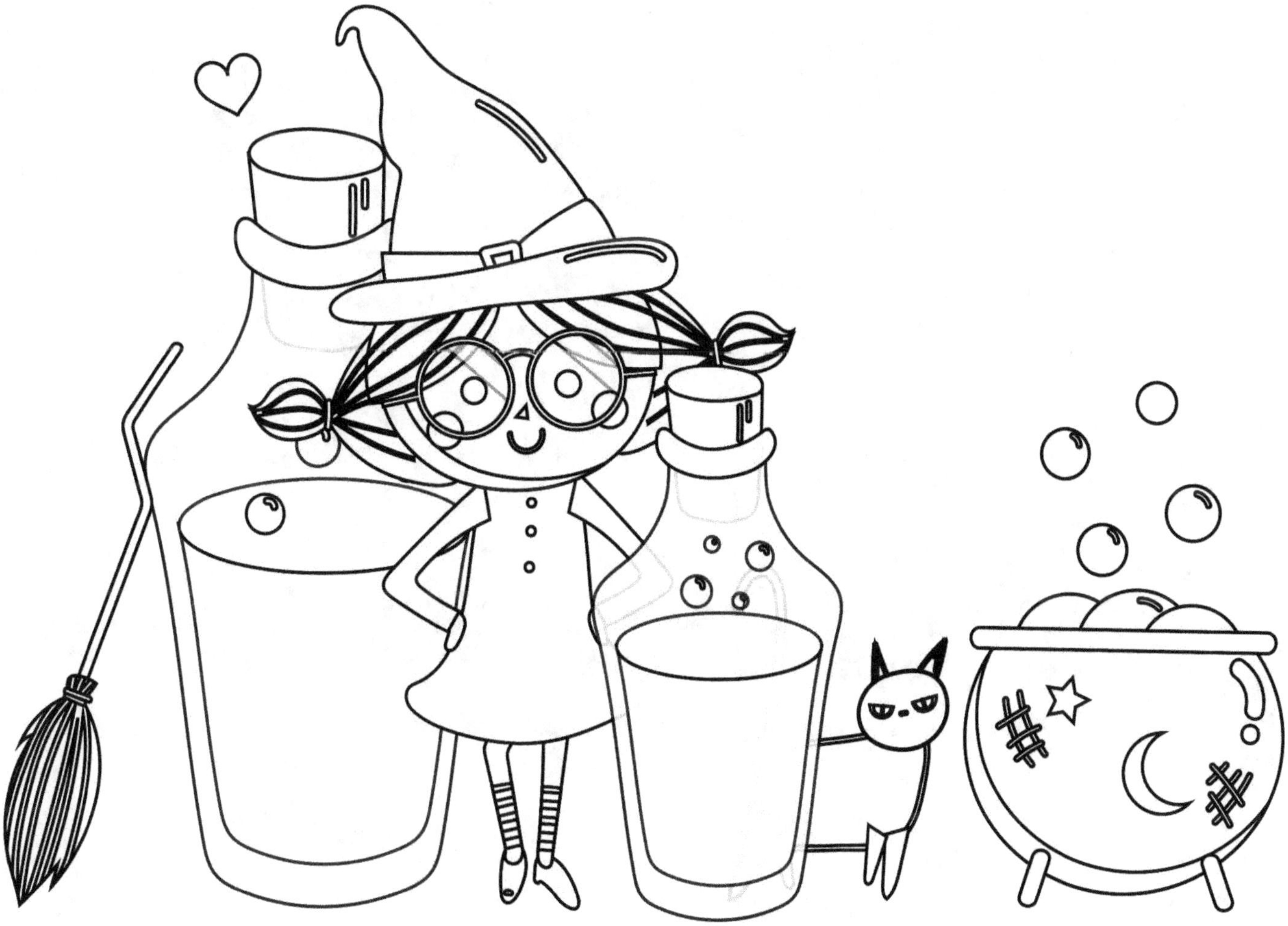

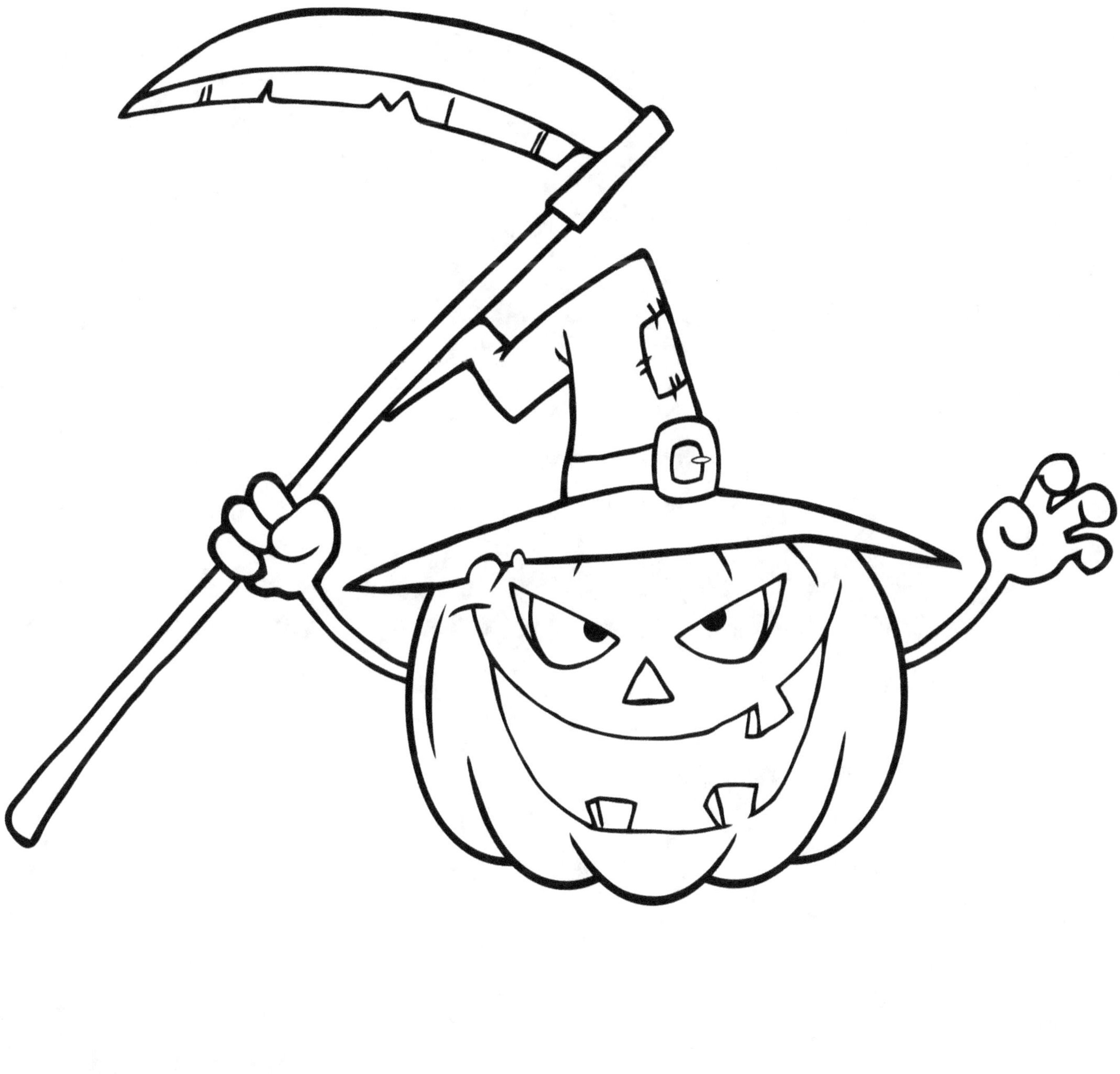

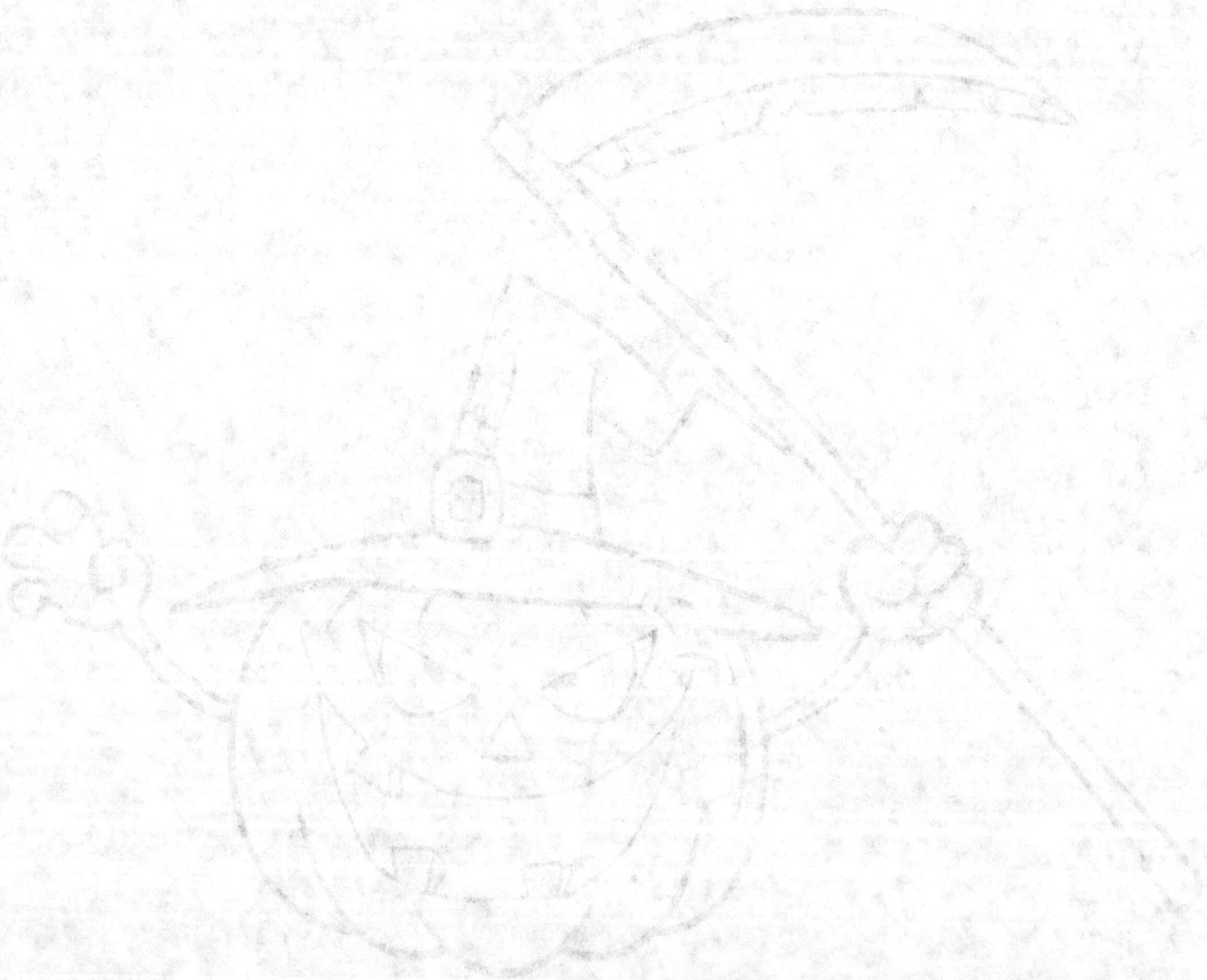

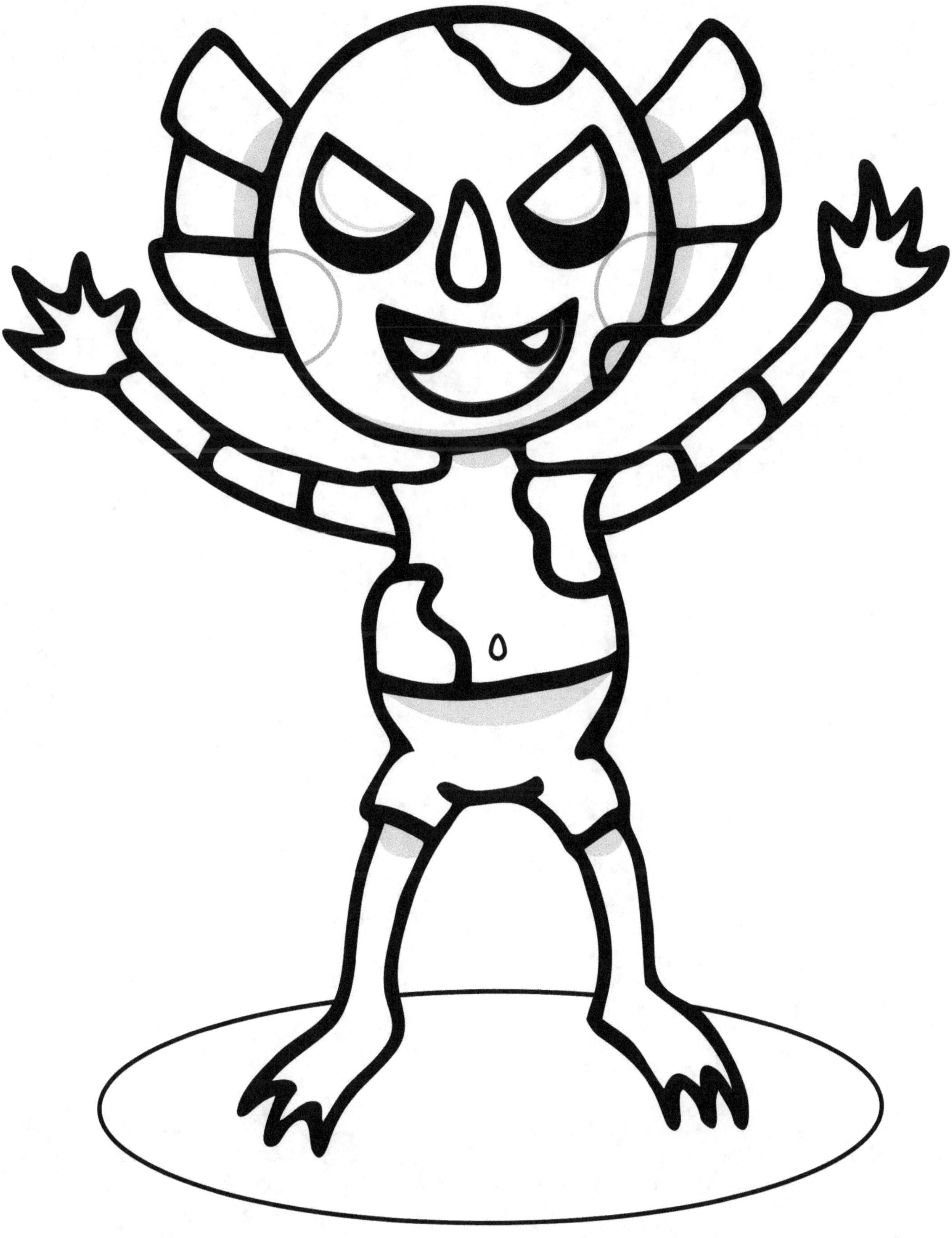

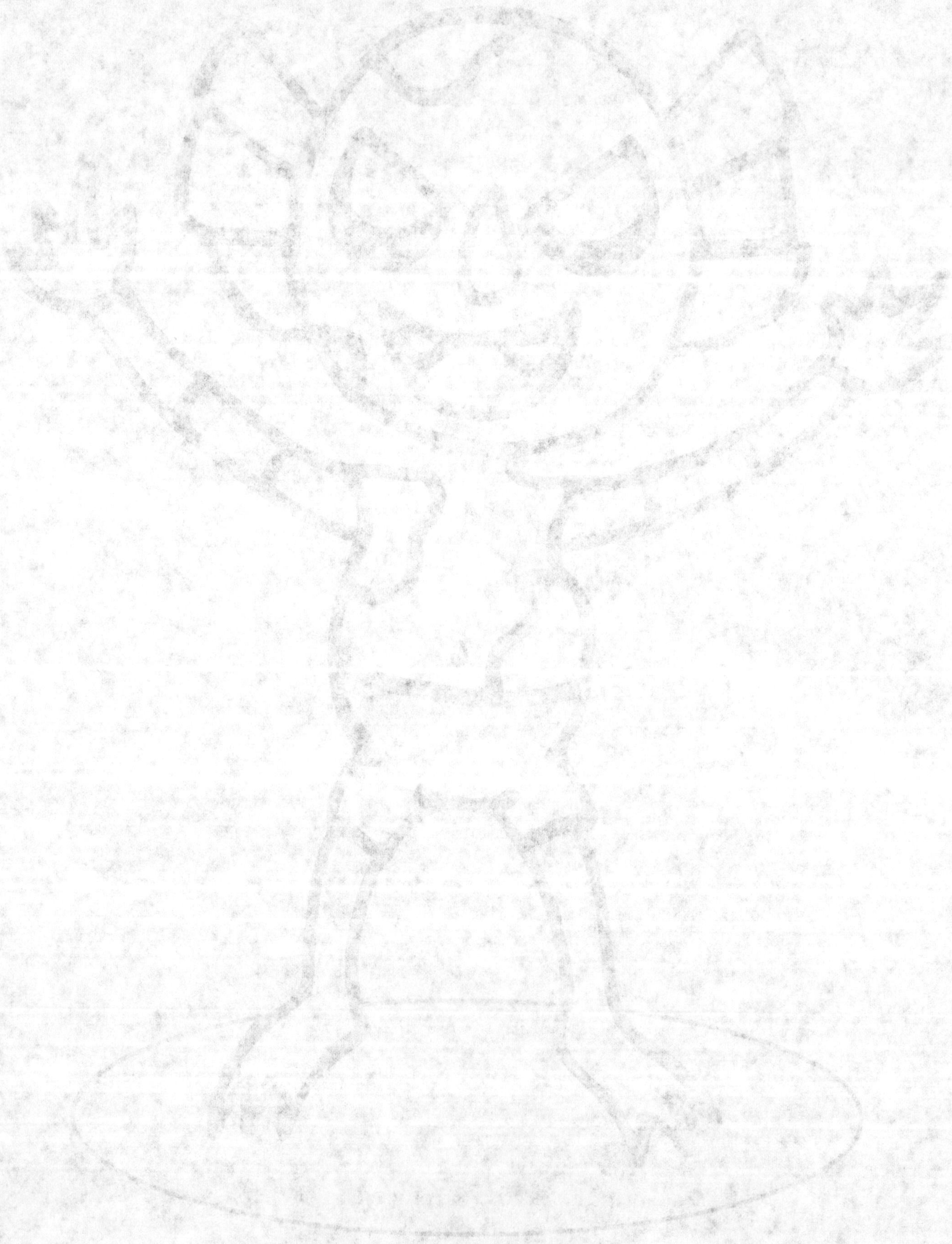

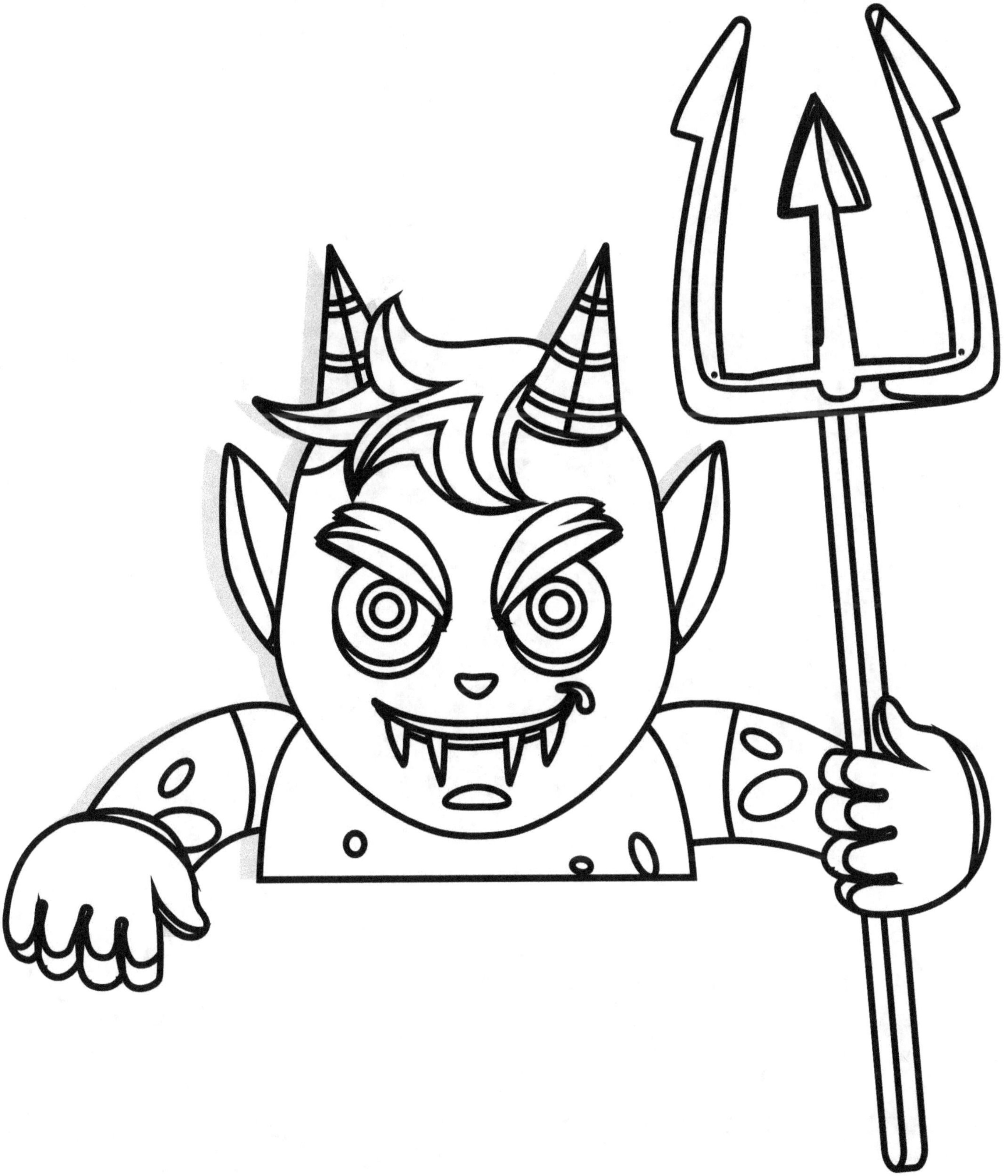

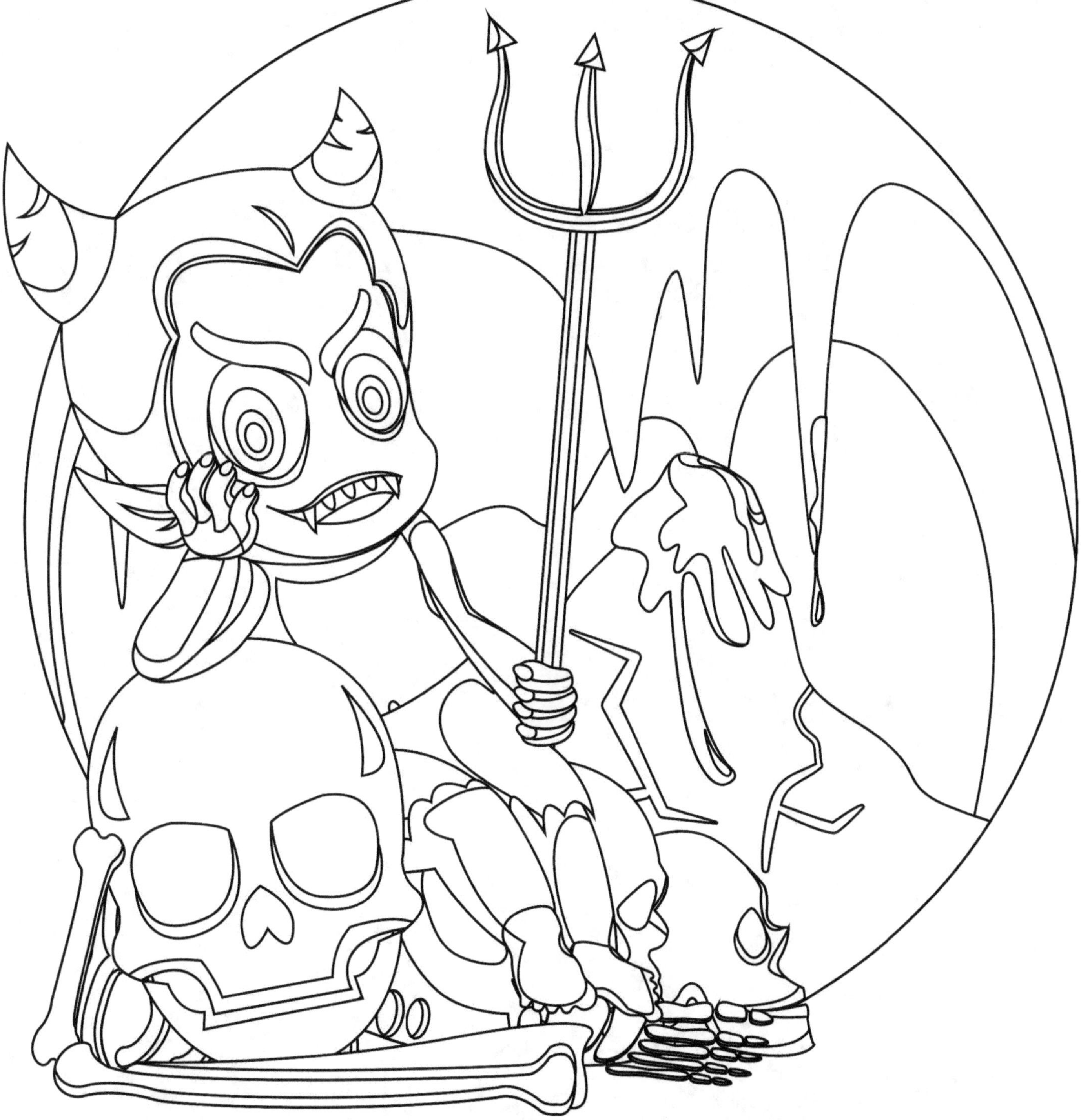

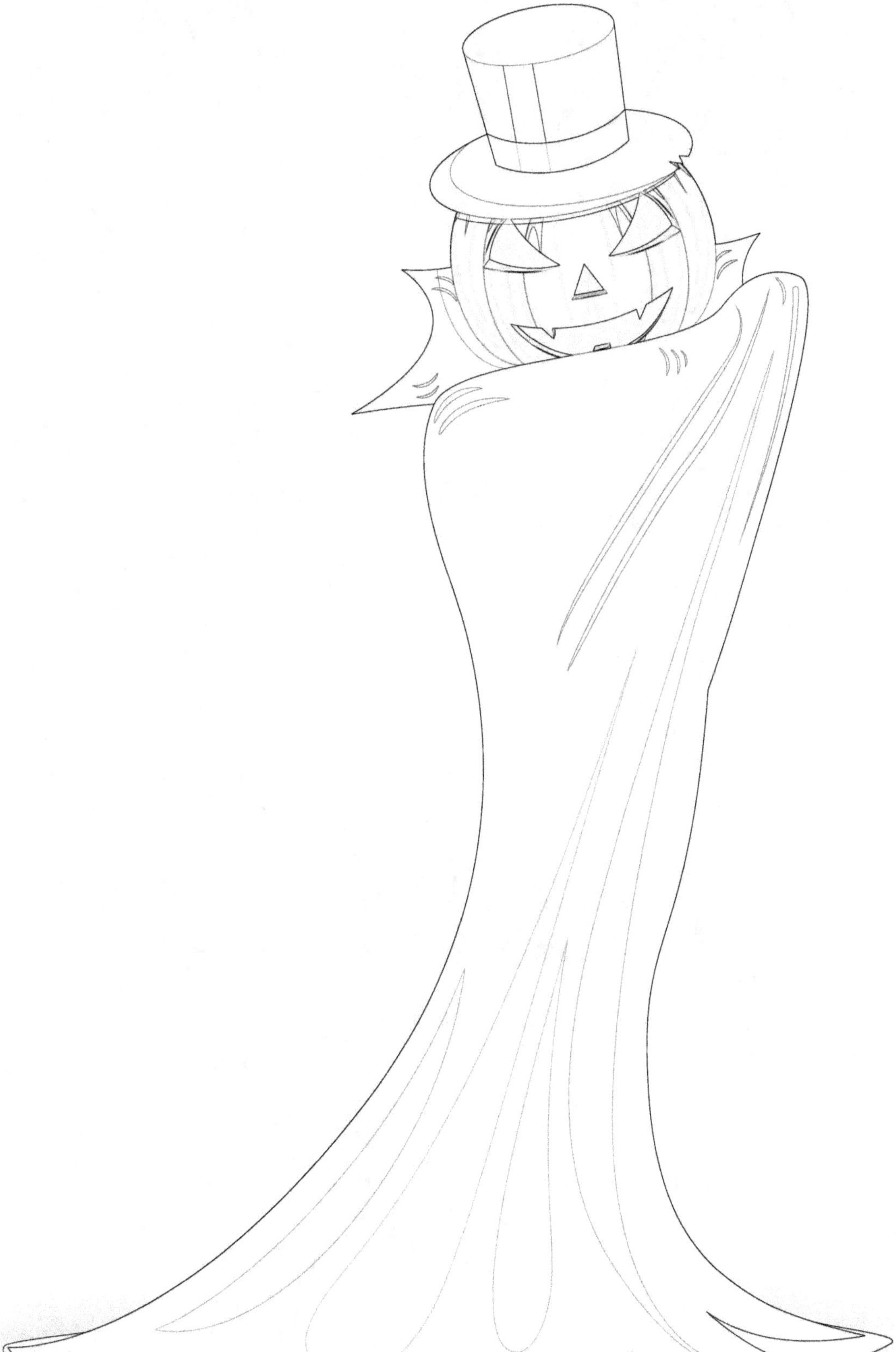

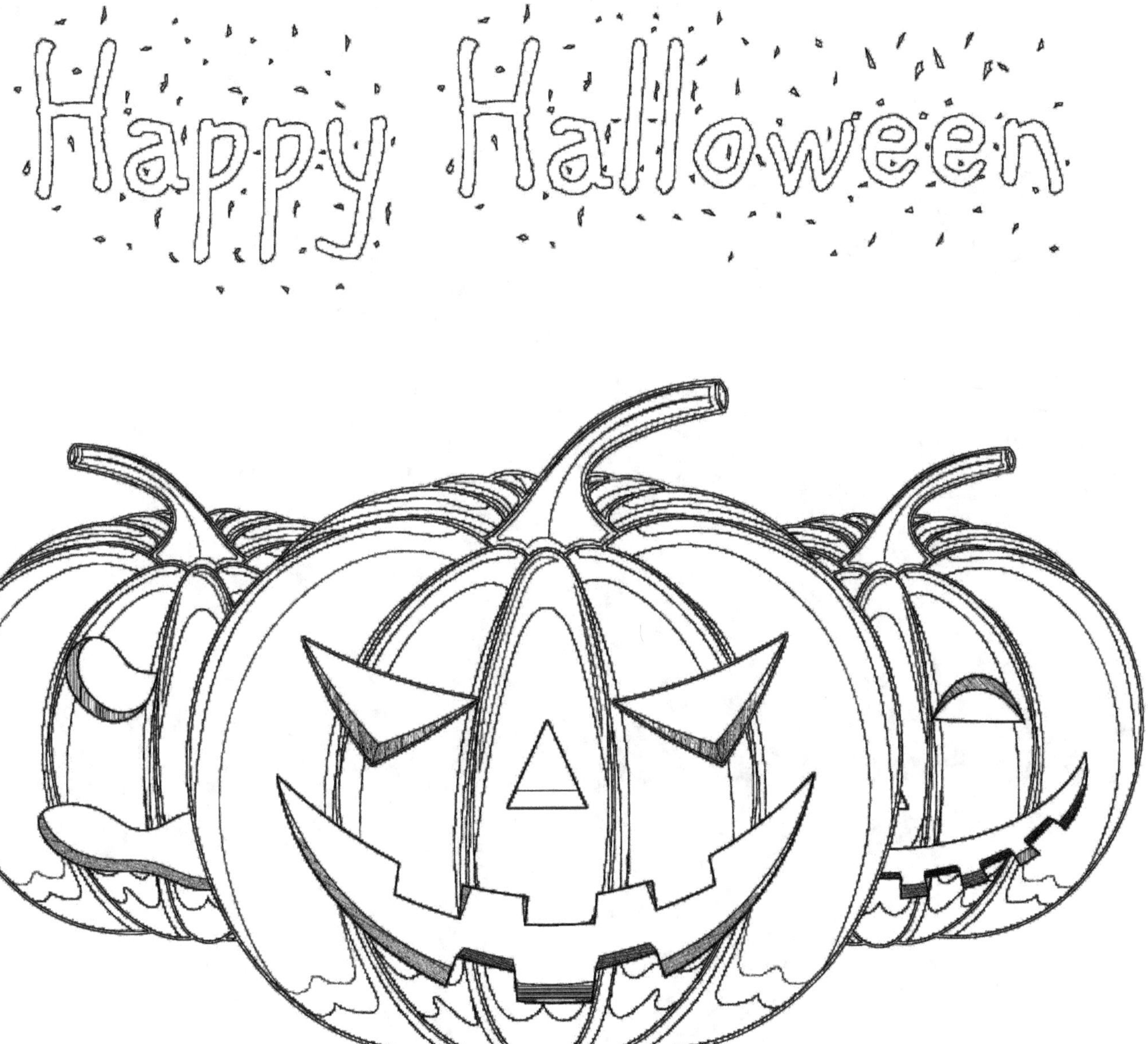
Happy Halloween

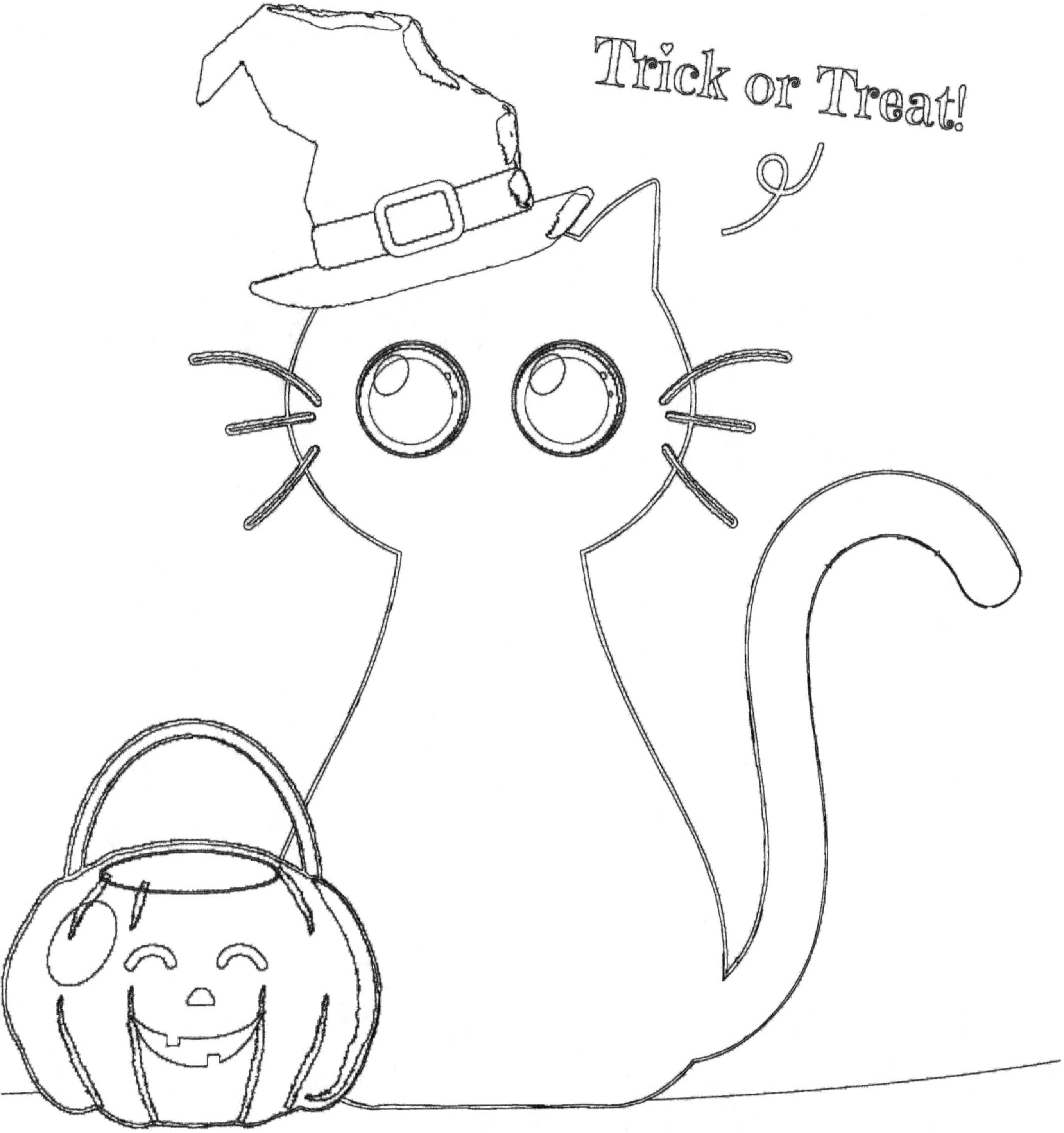
Trick or Treat!

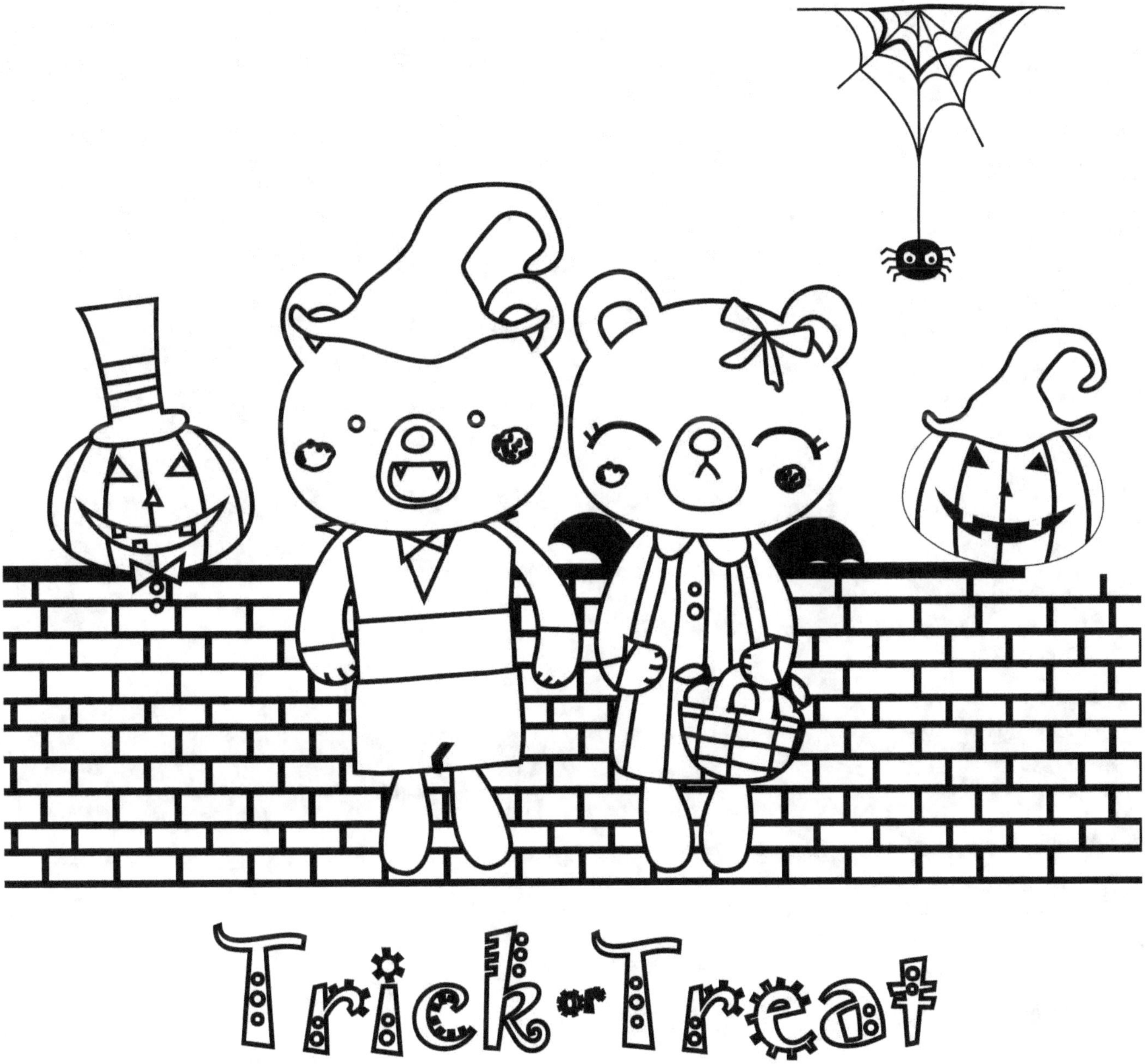
Trick or Treat

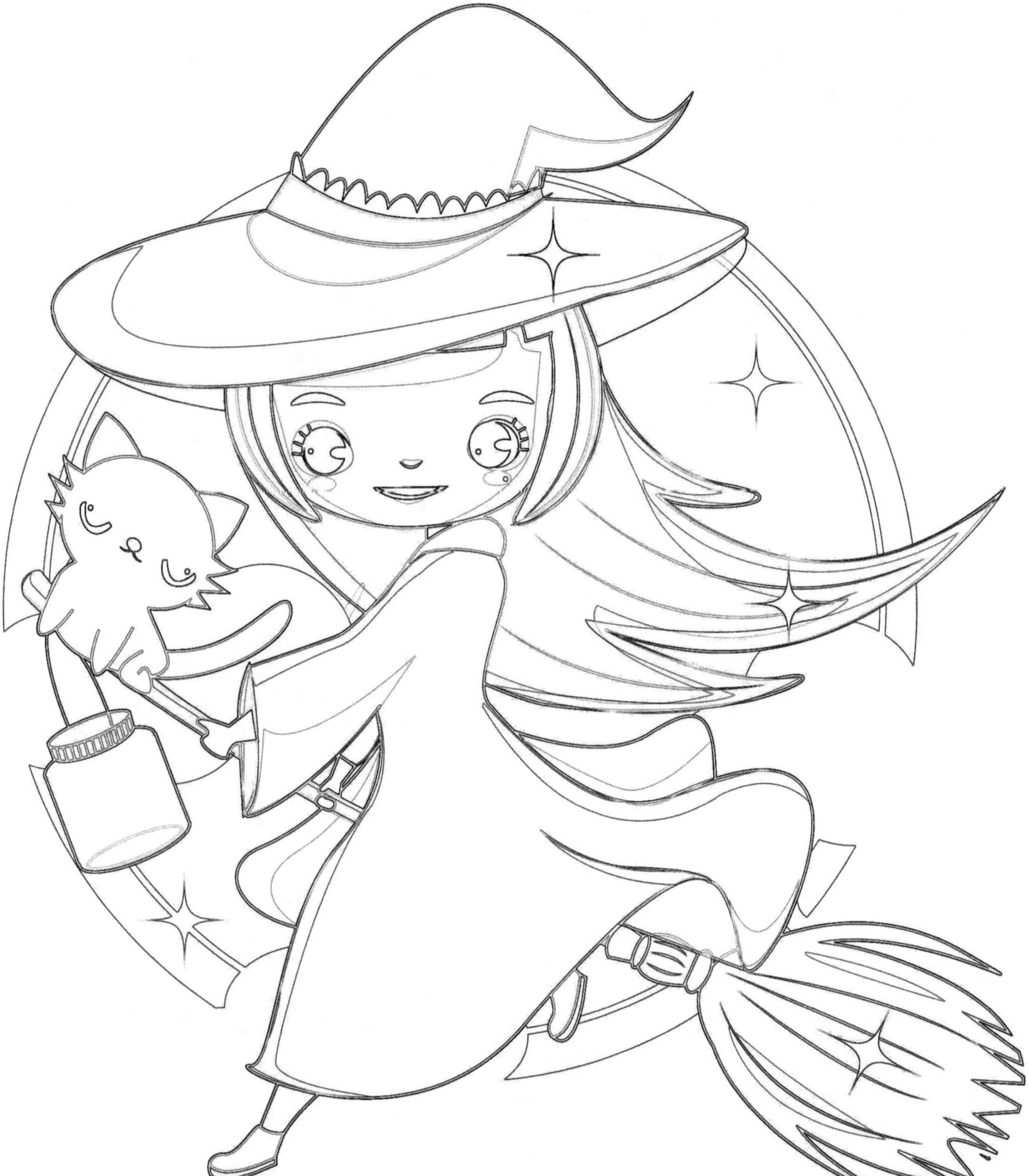

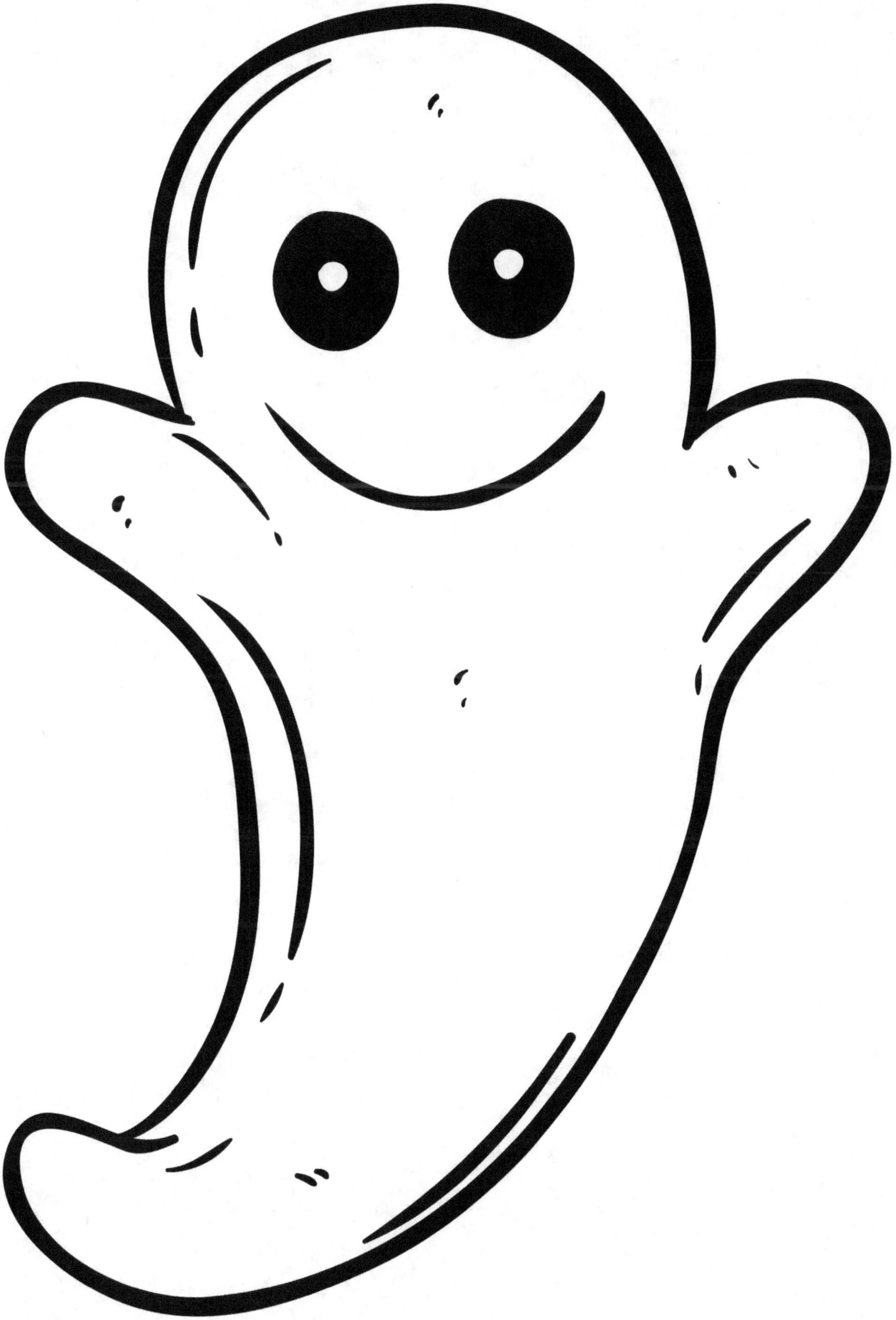

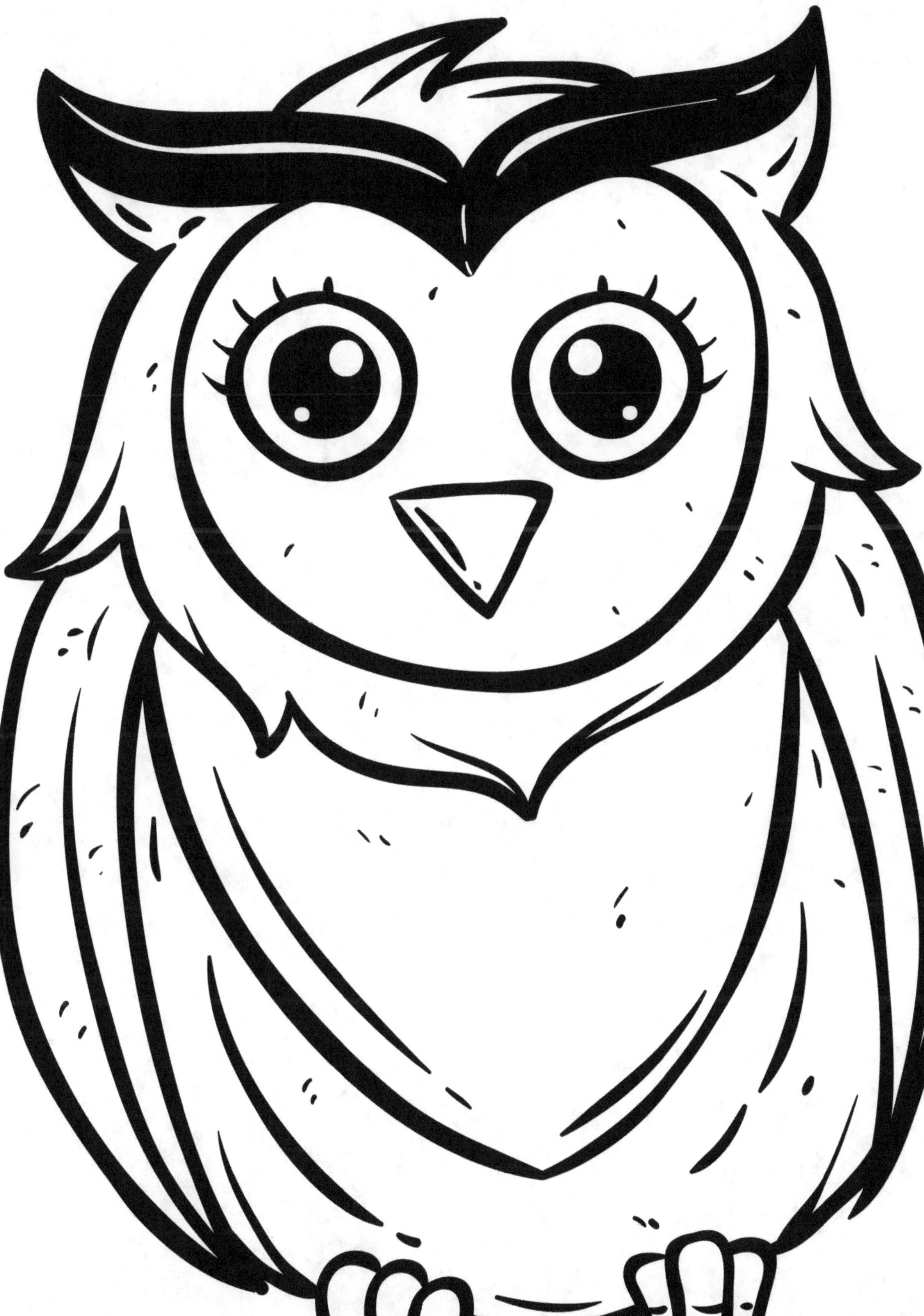

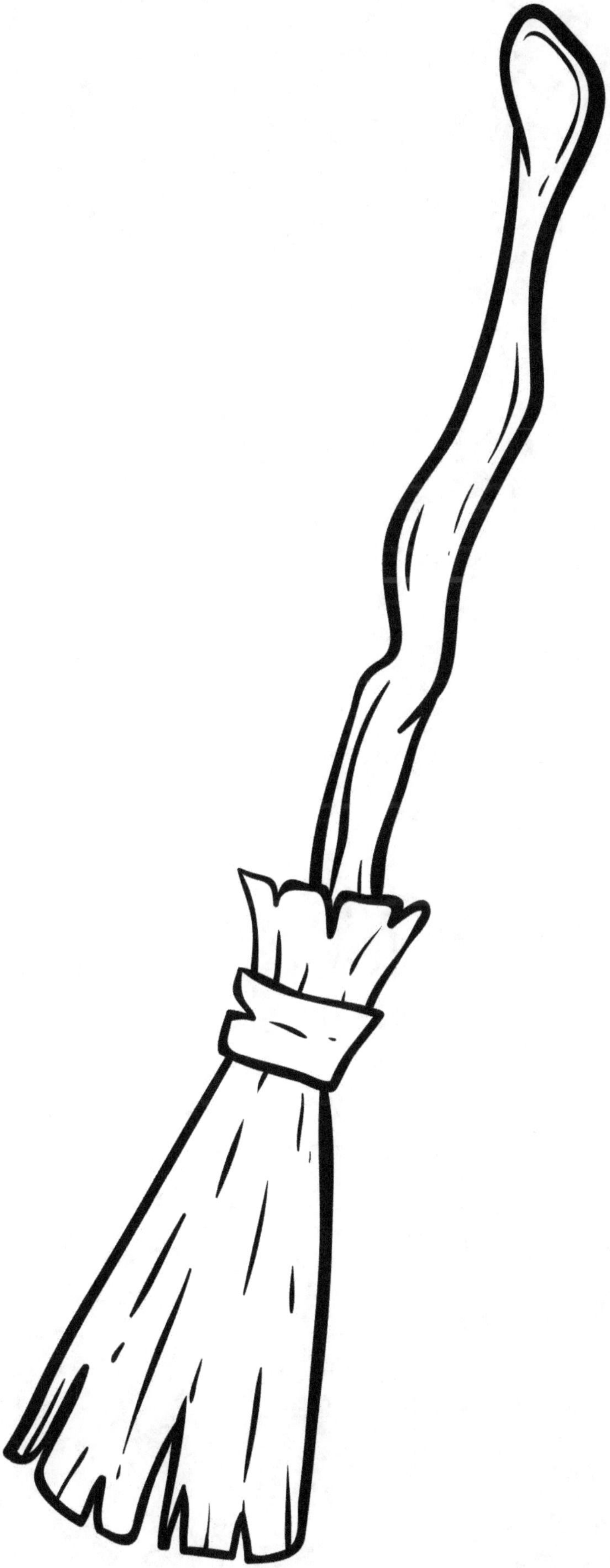

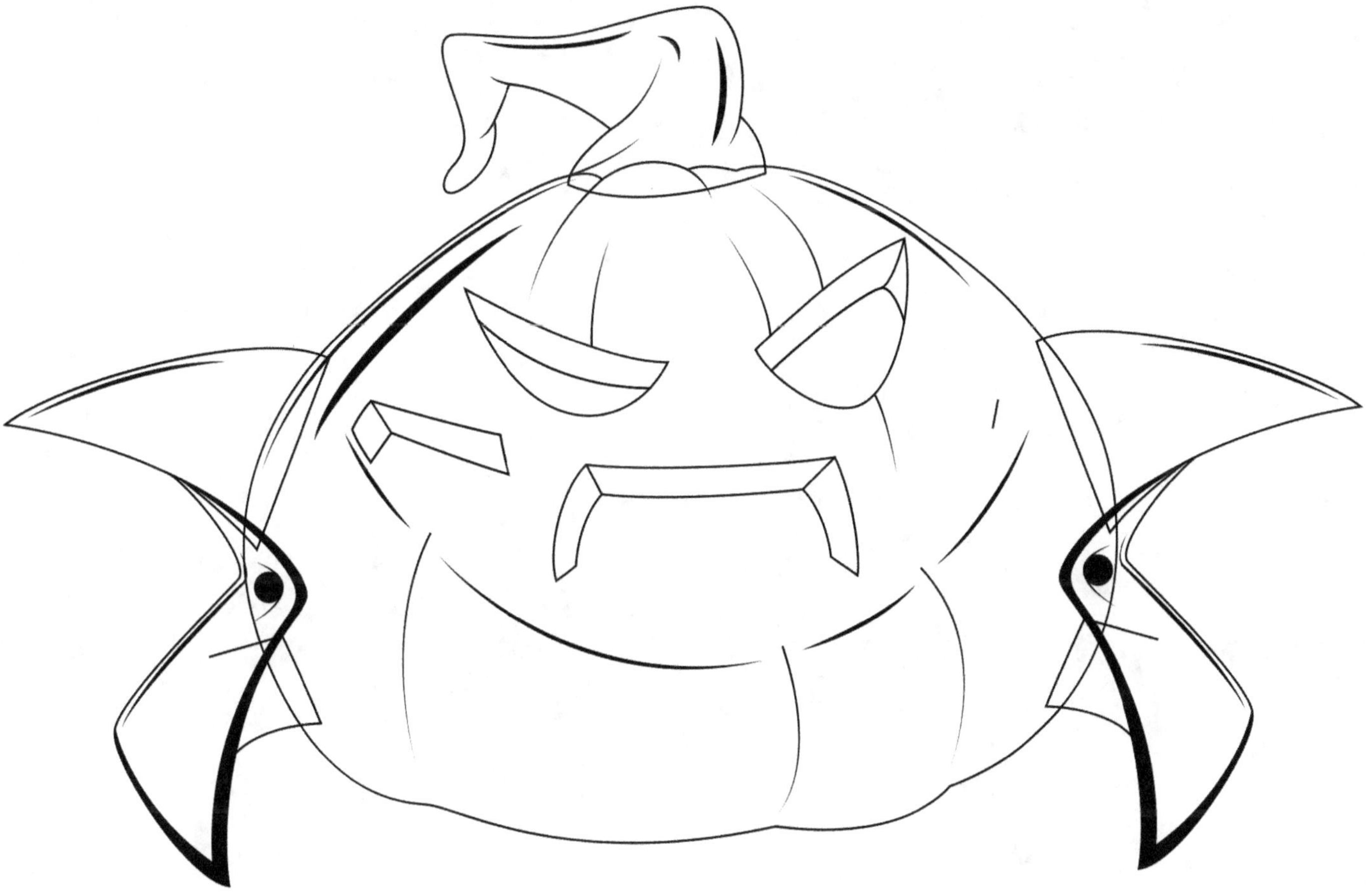

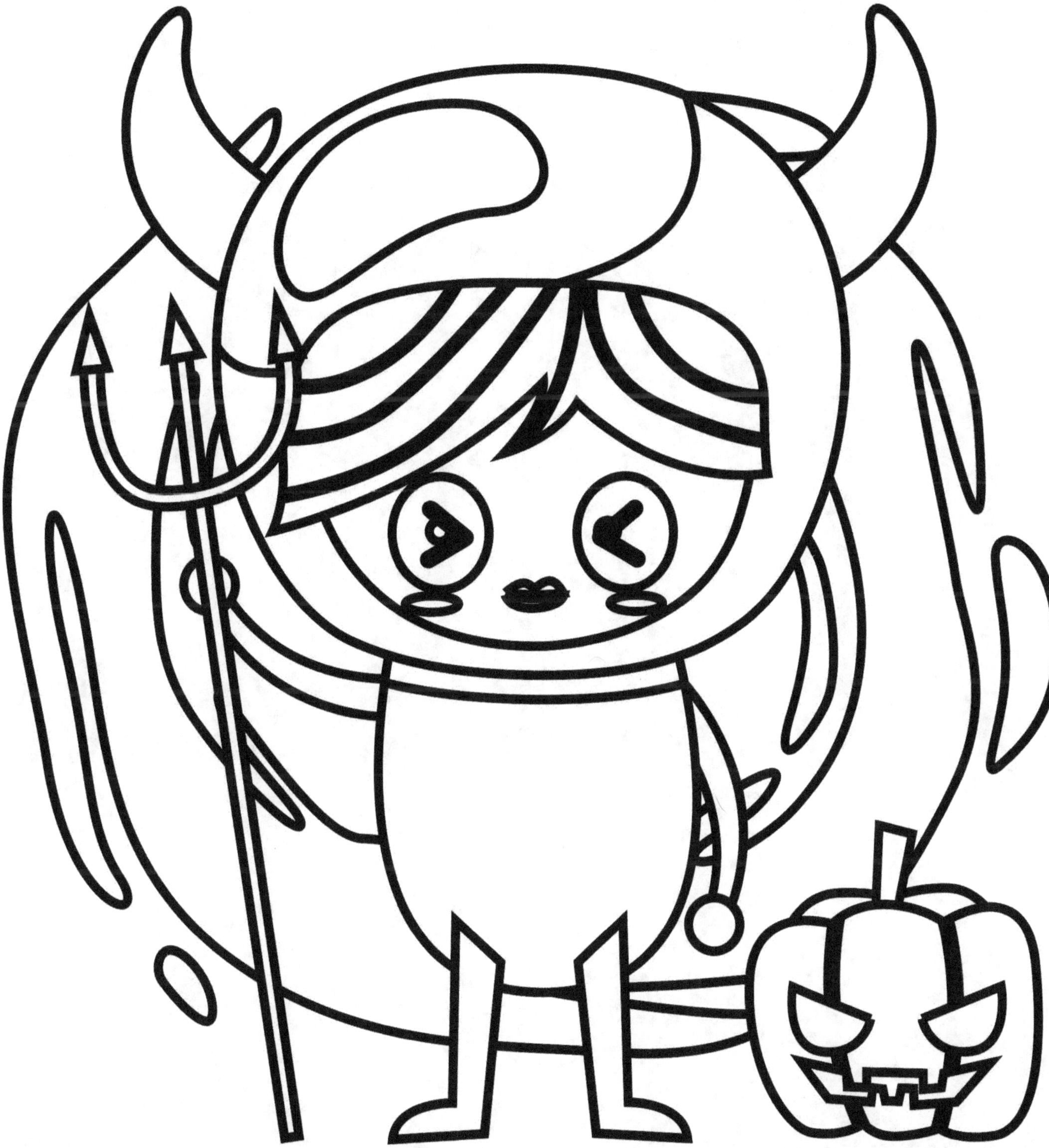

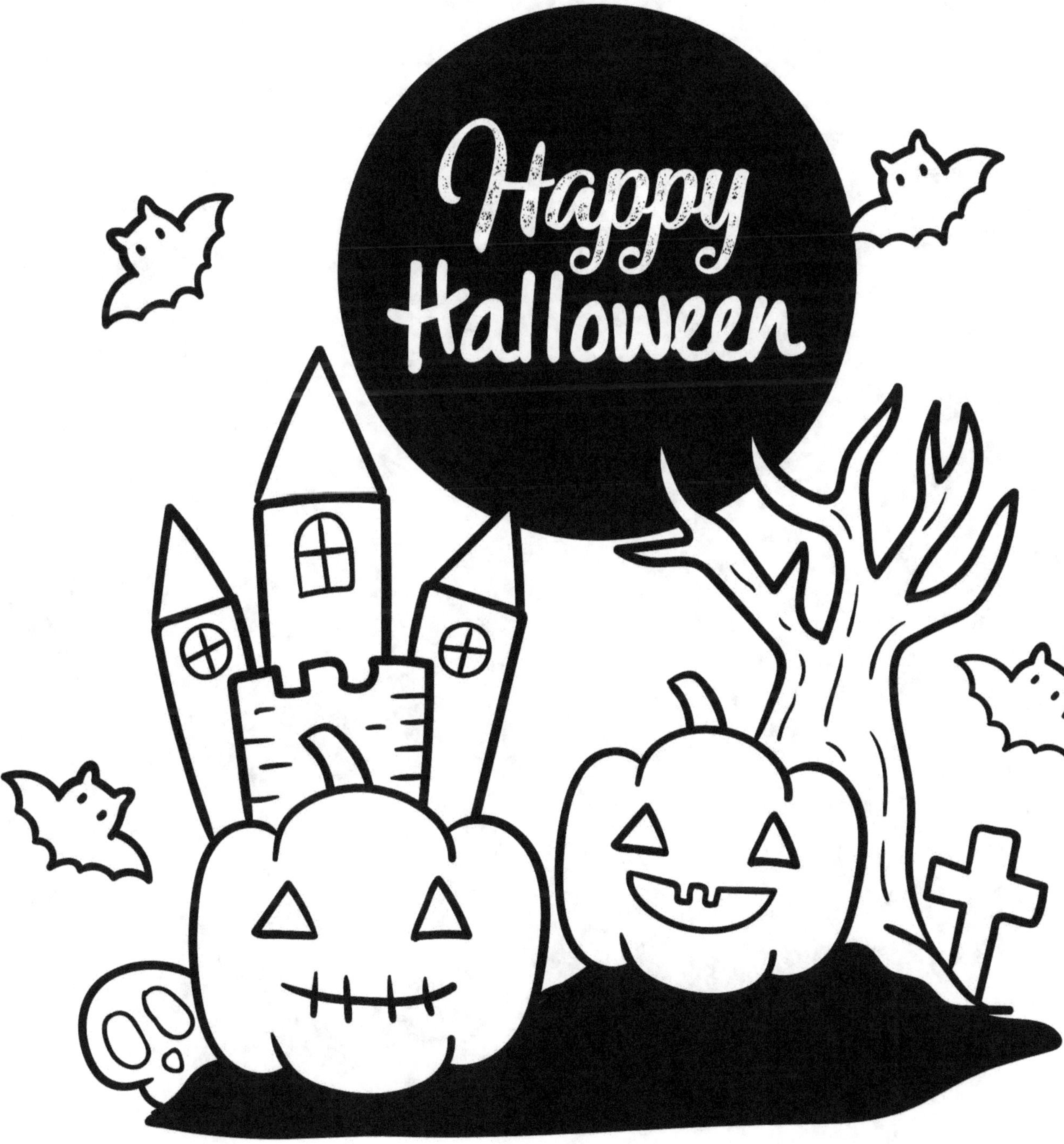
Happy
Halloween

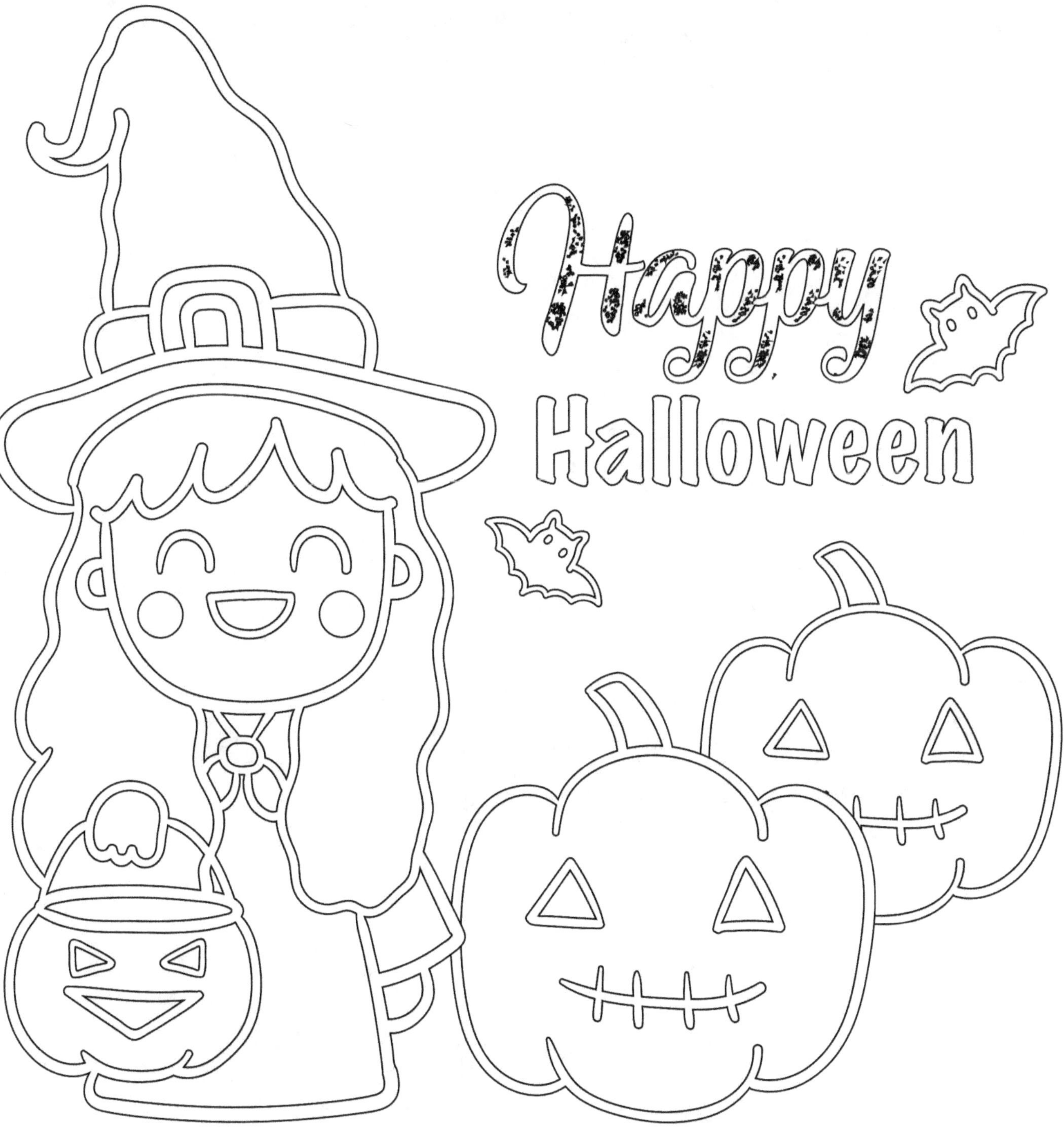
Happy
Halloween

Halloween
Party

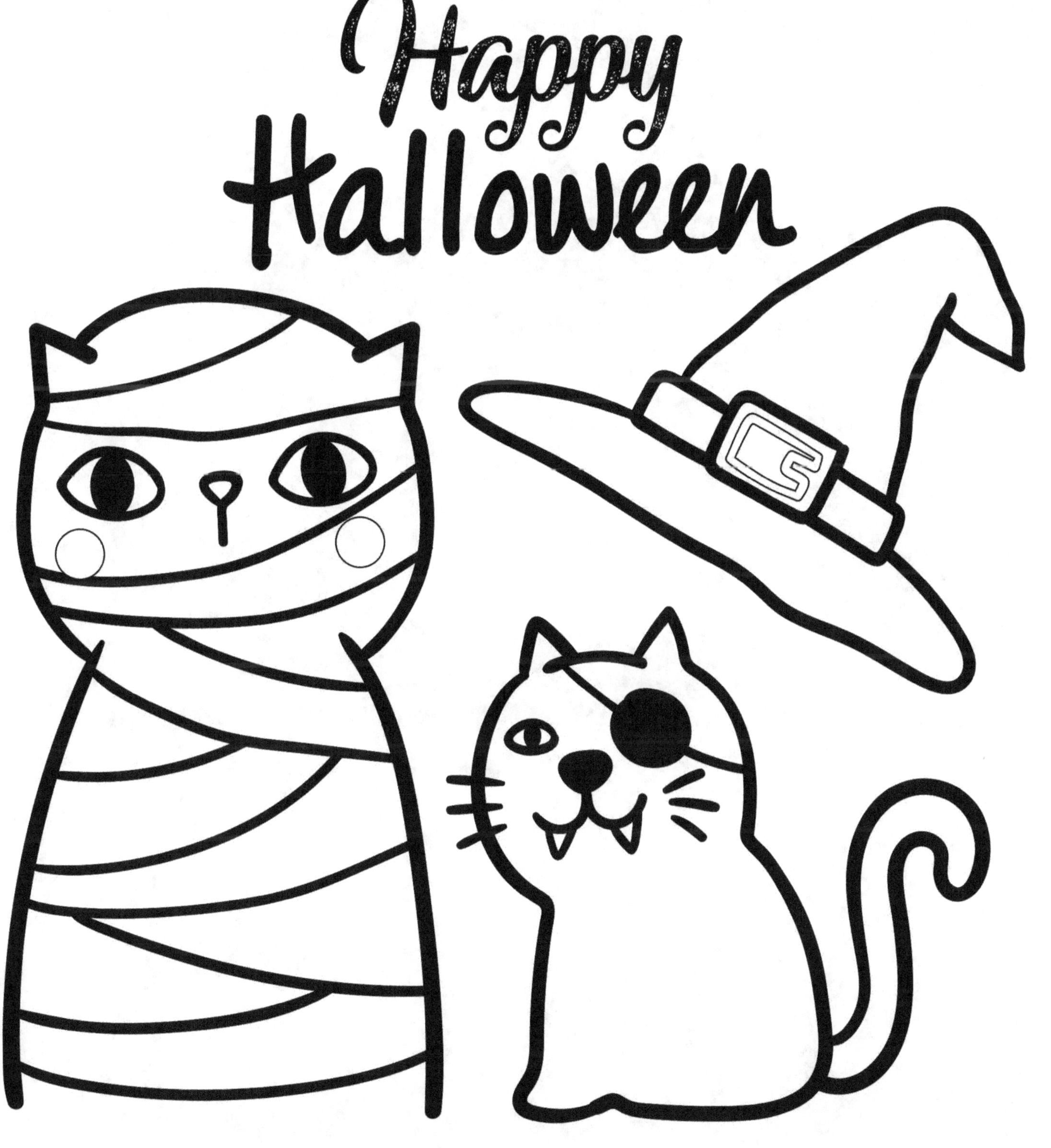
Happy
Halloween

Halloween
Party
RIP

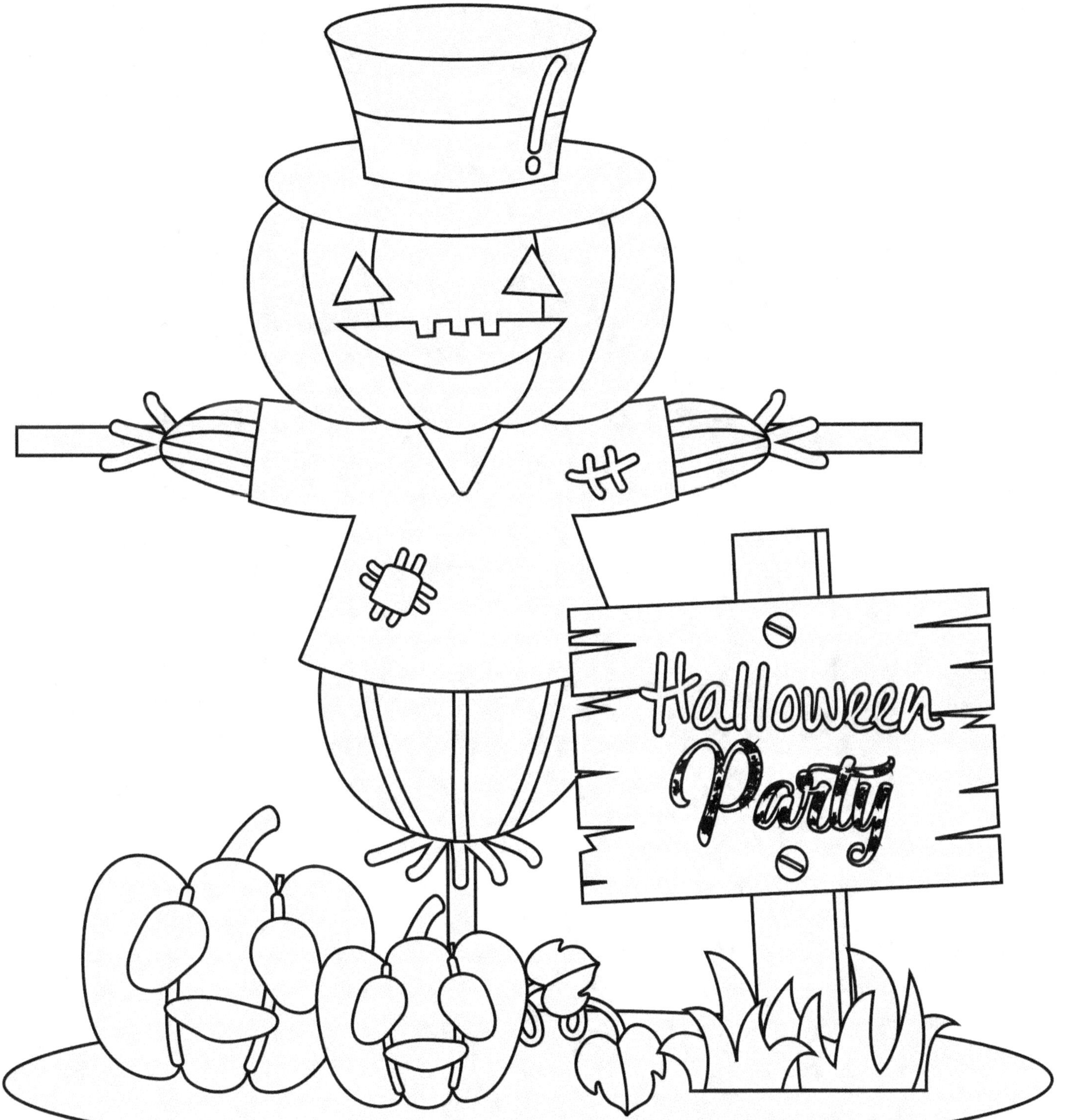
Halloween
Party

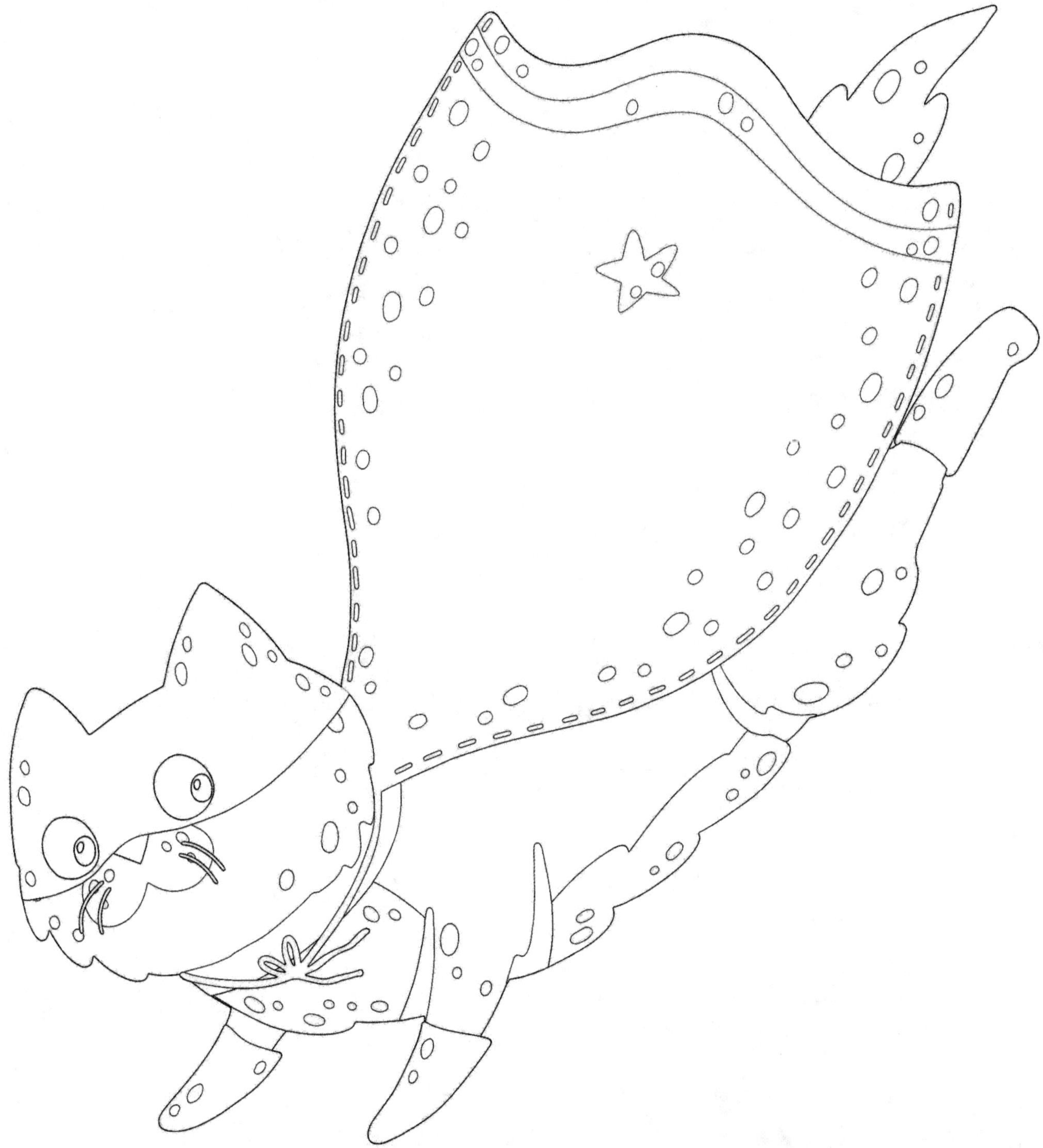

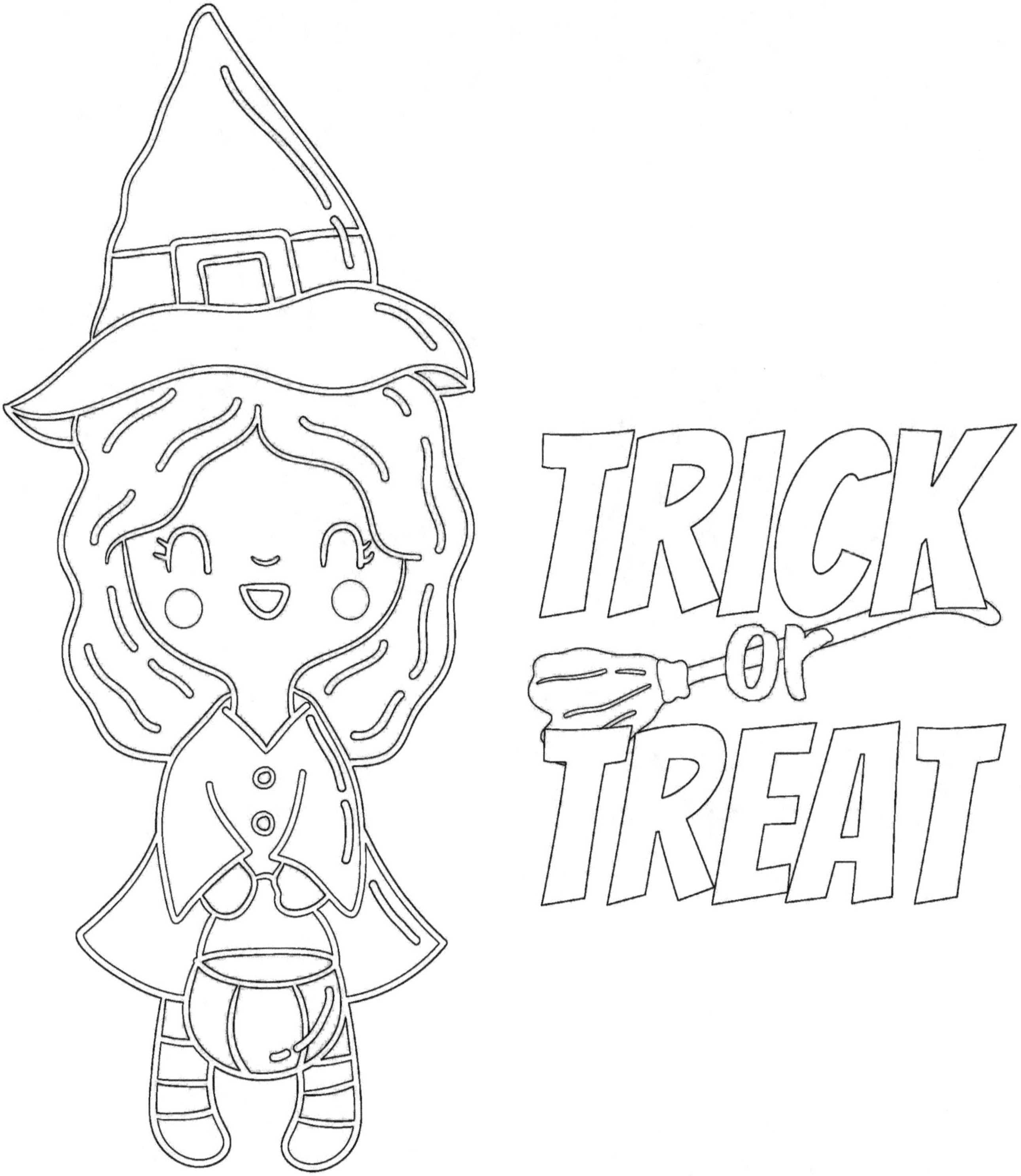
TRICK
or
TREAT

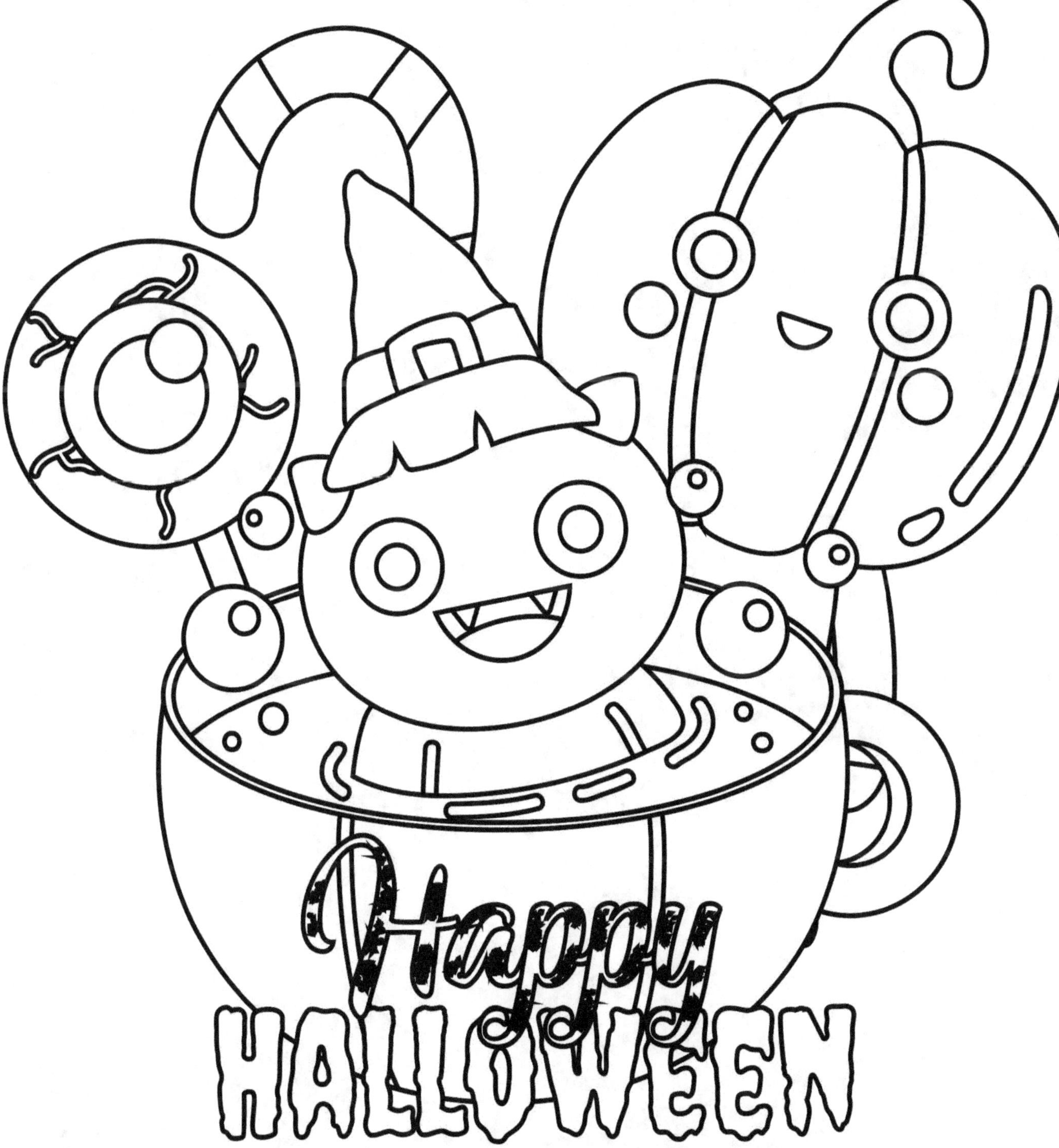
Happy
HALLOWEEN

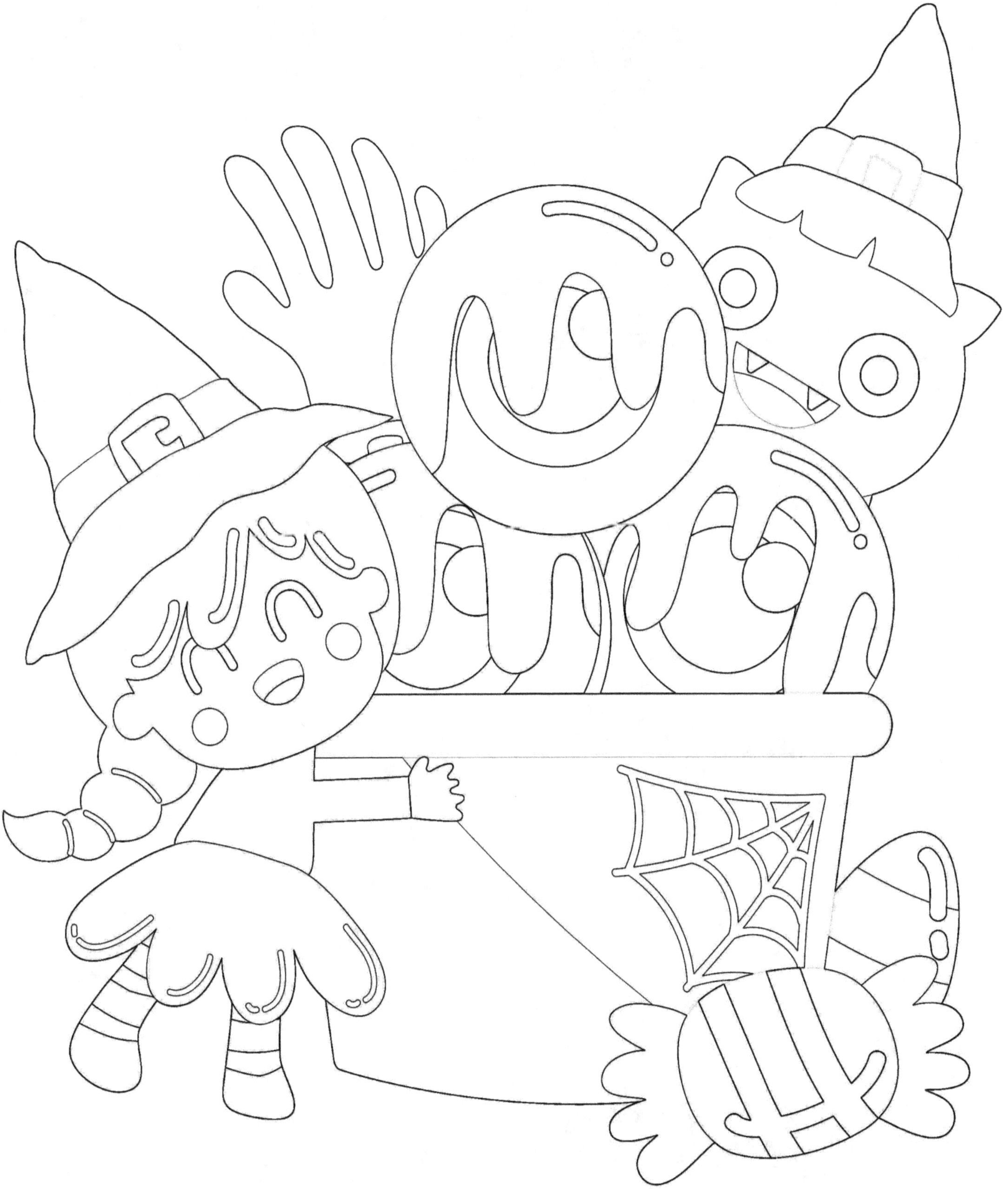

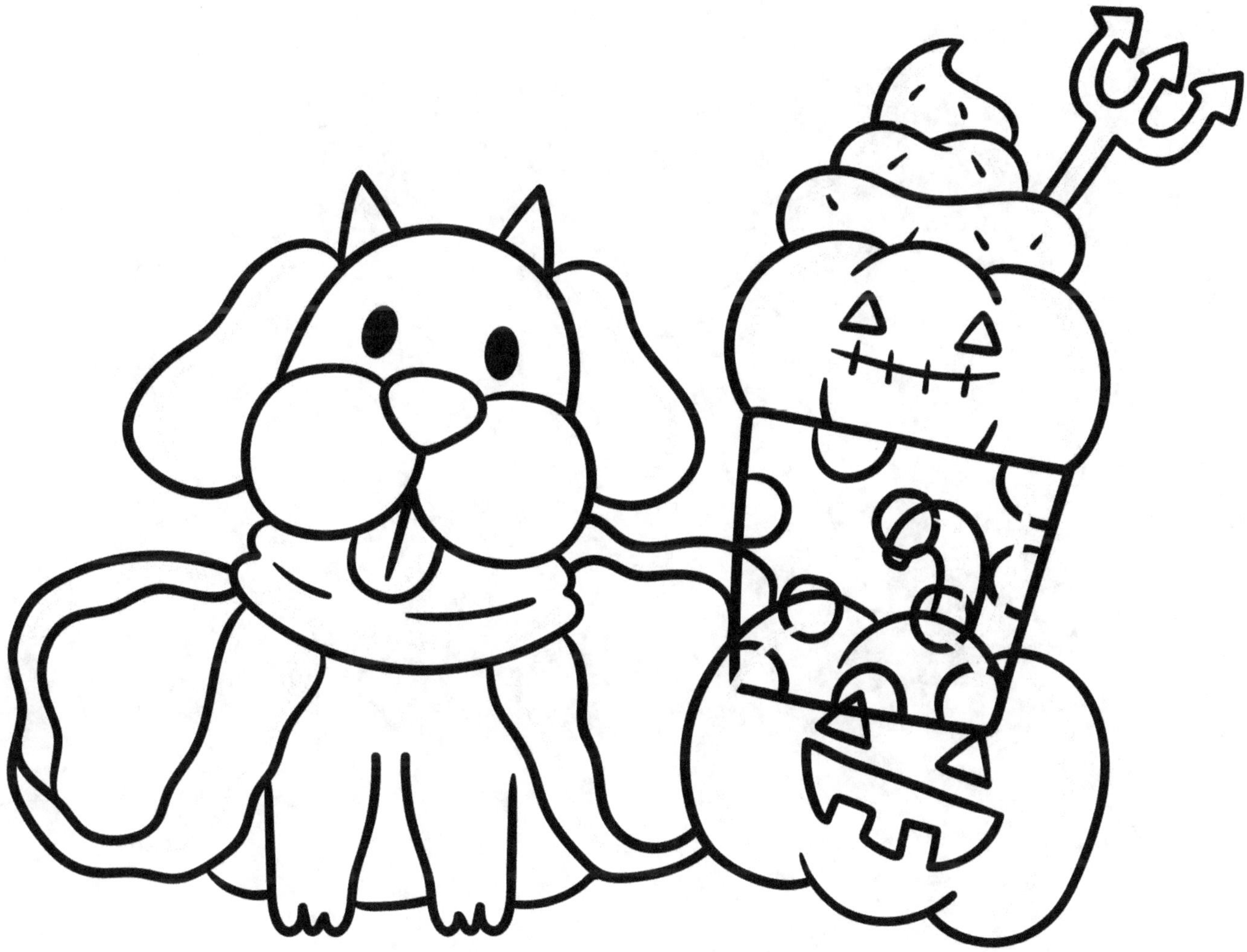

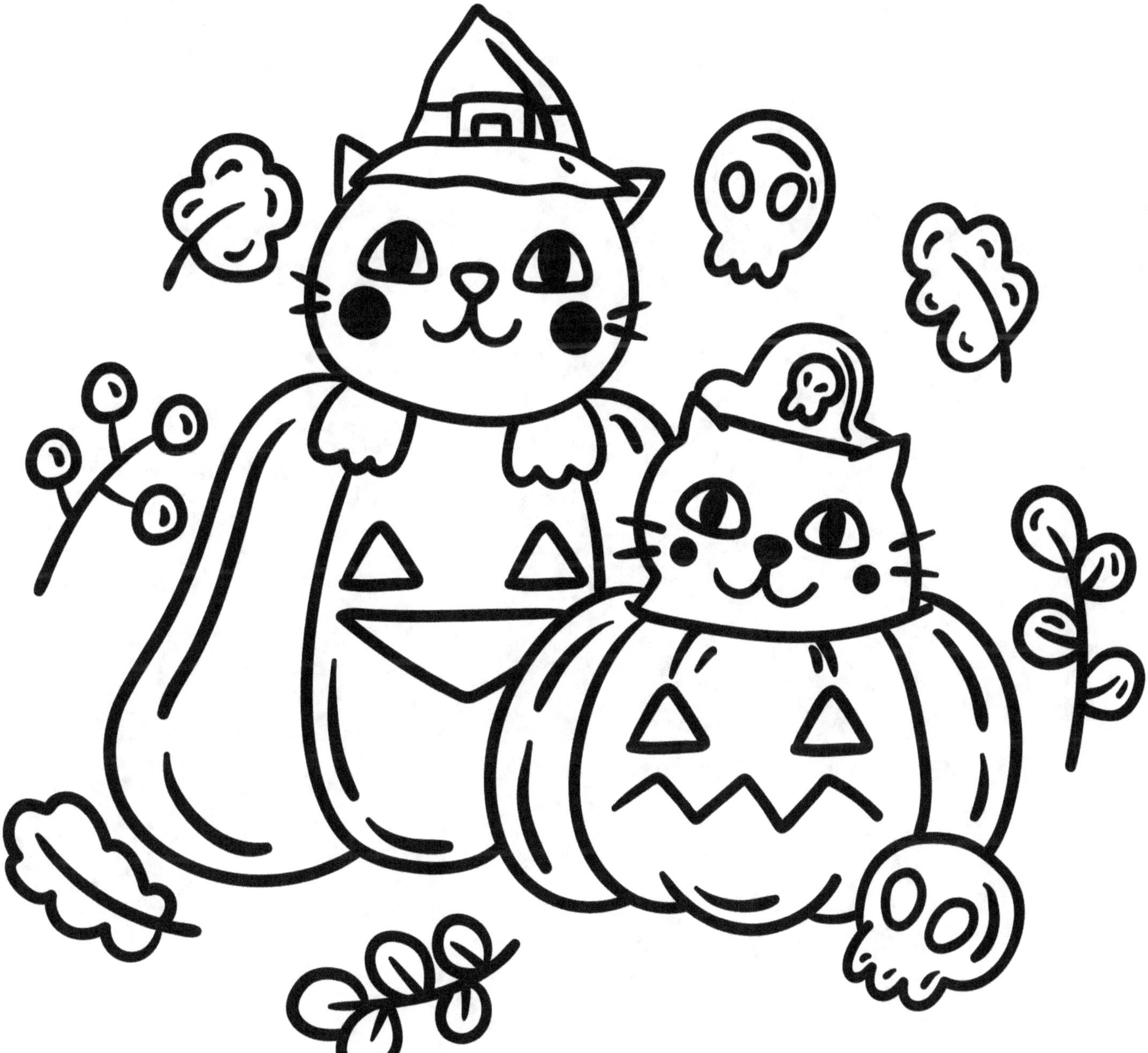

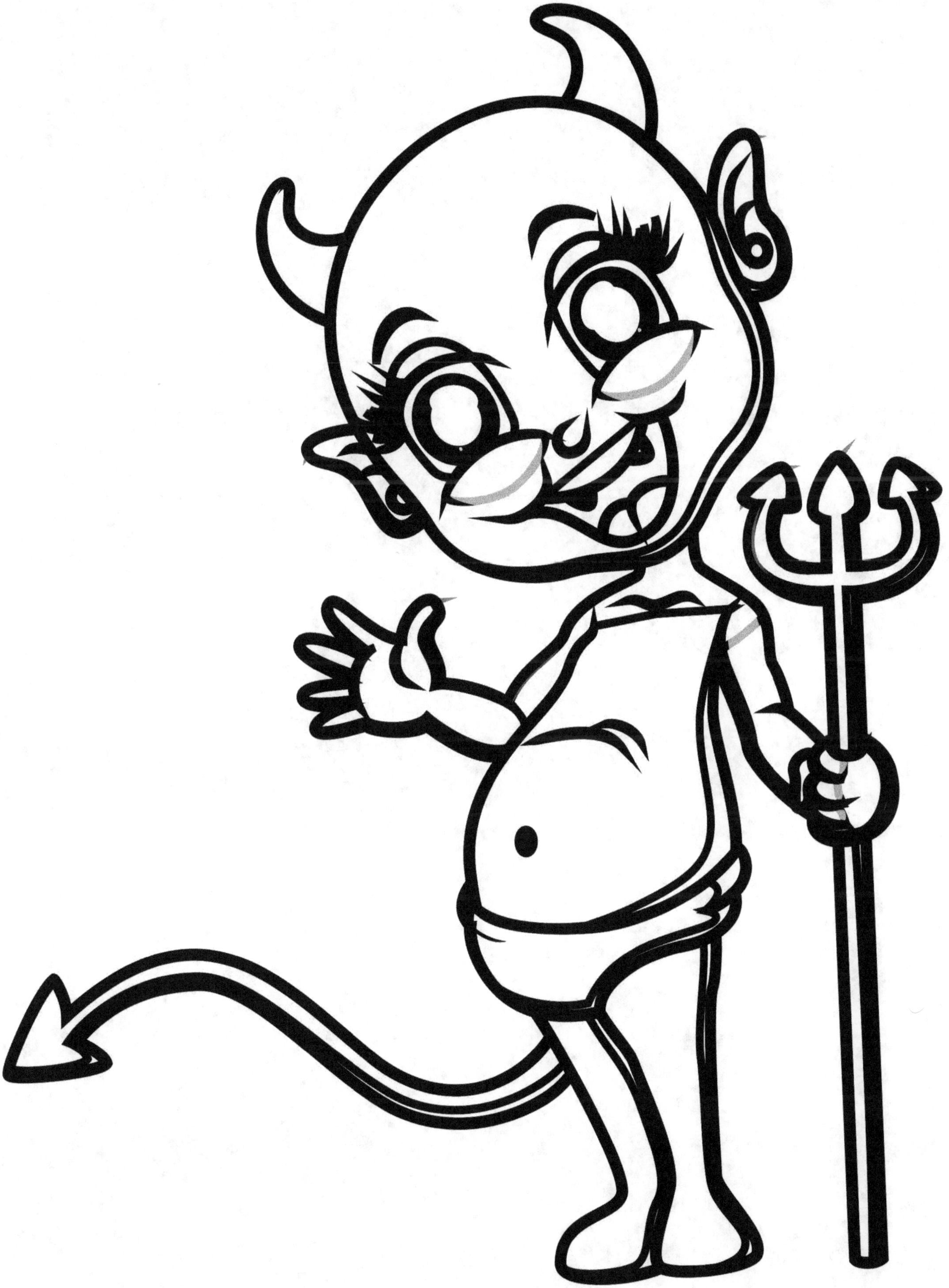

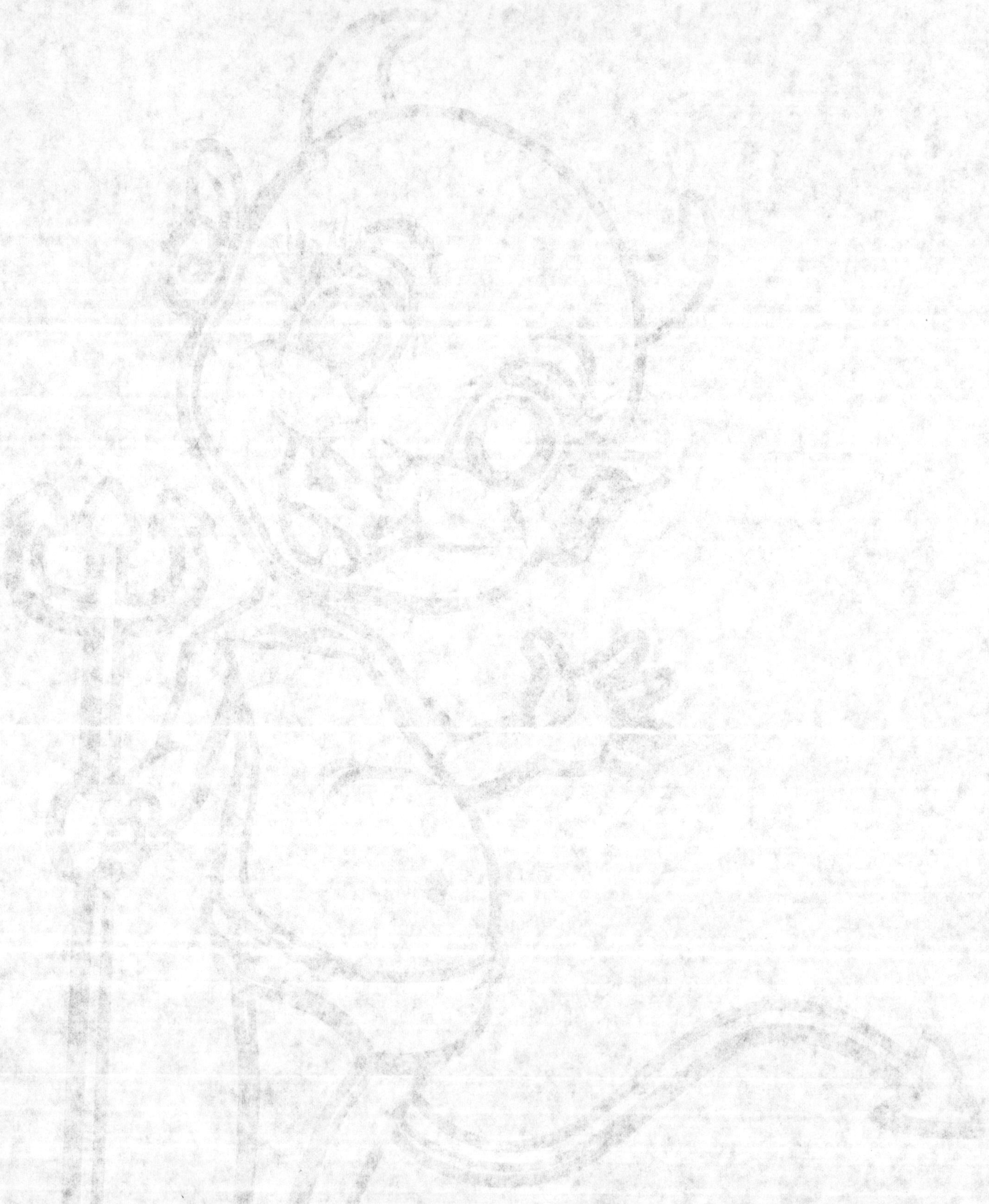

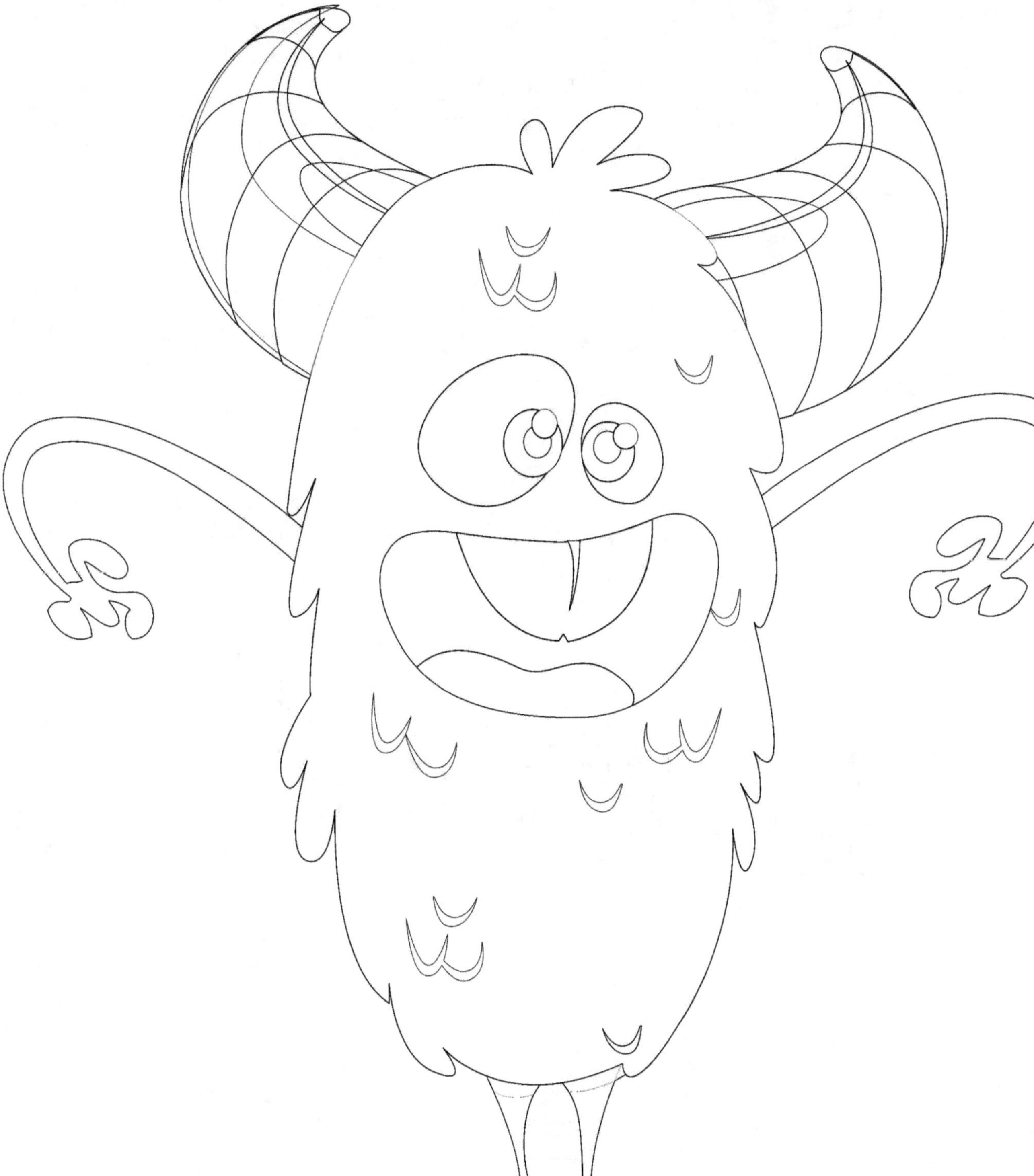

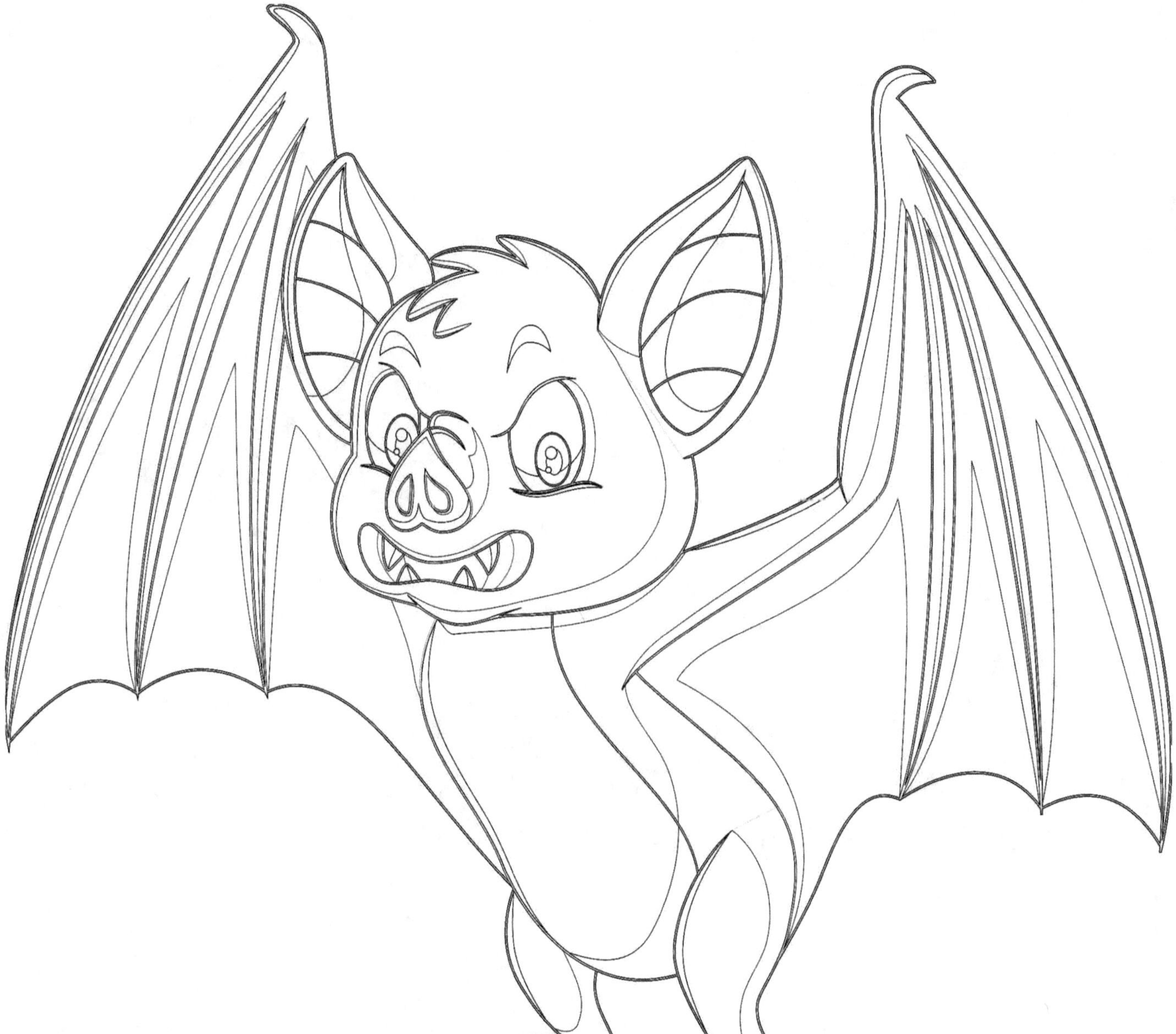

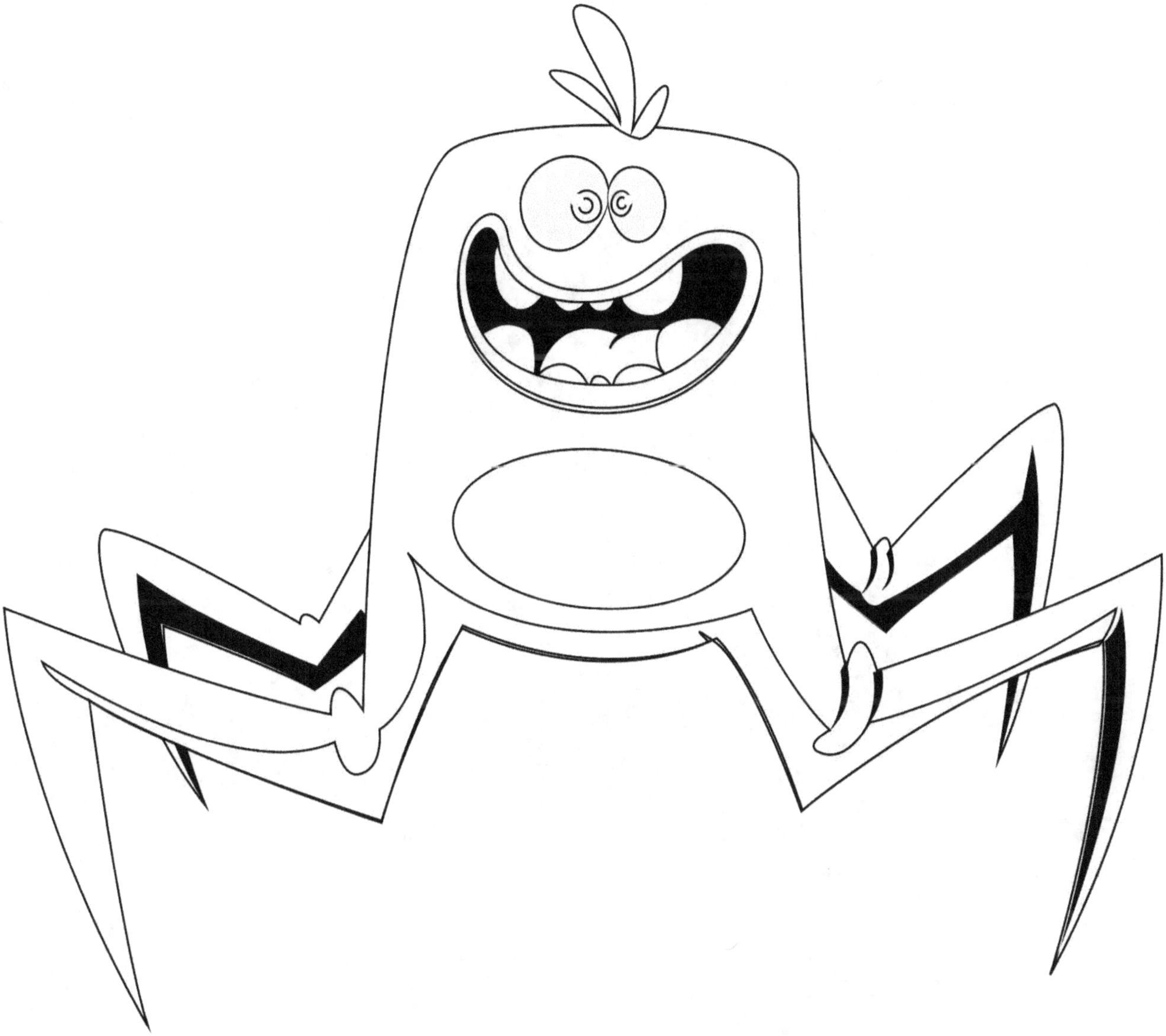

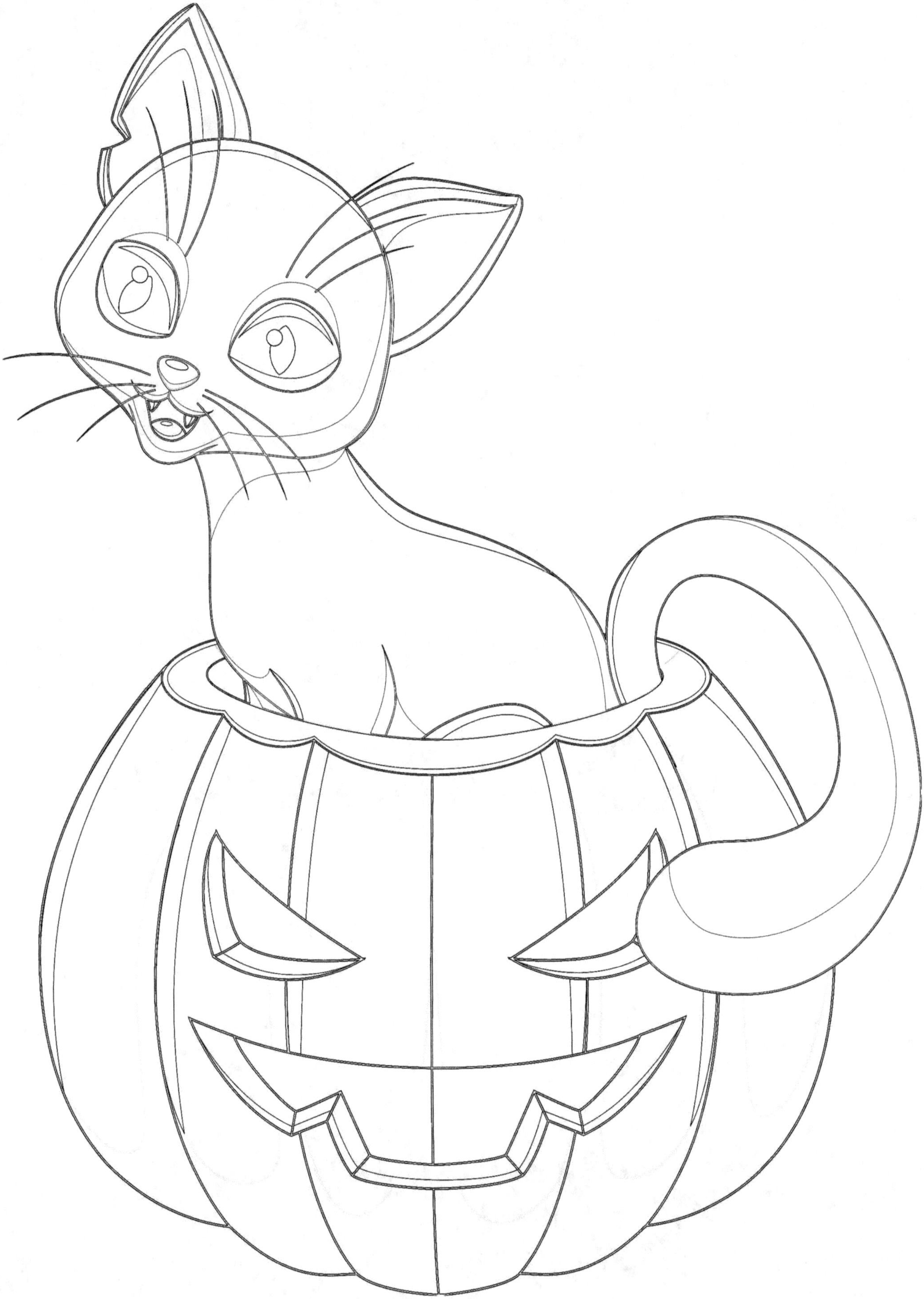

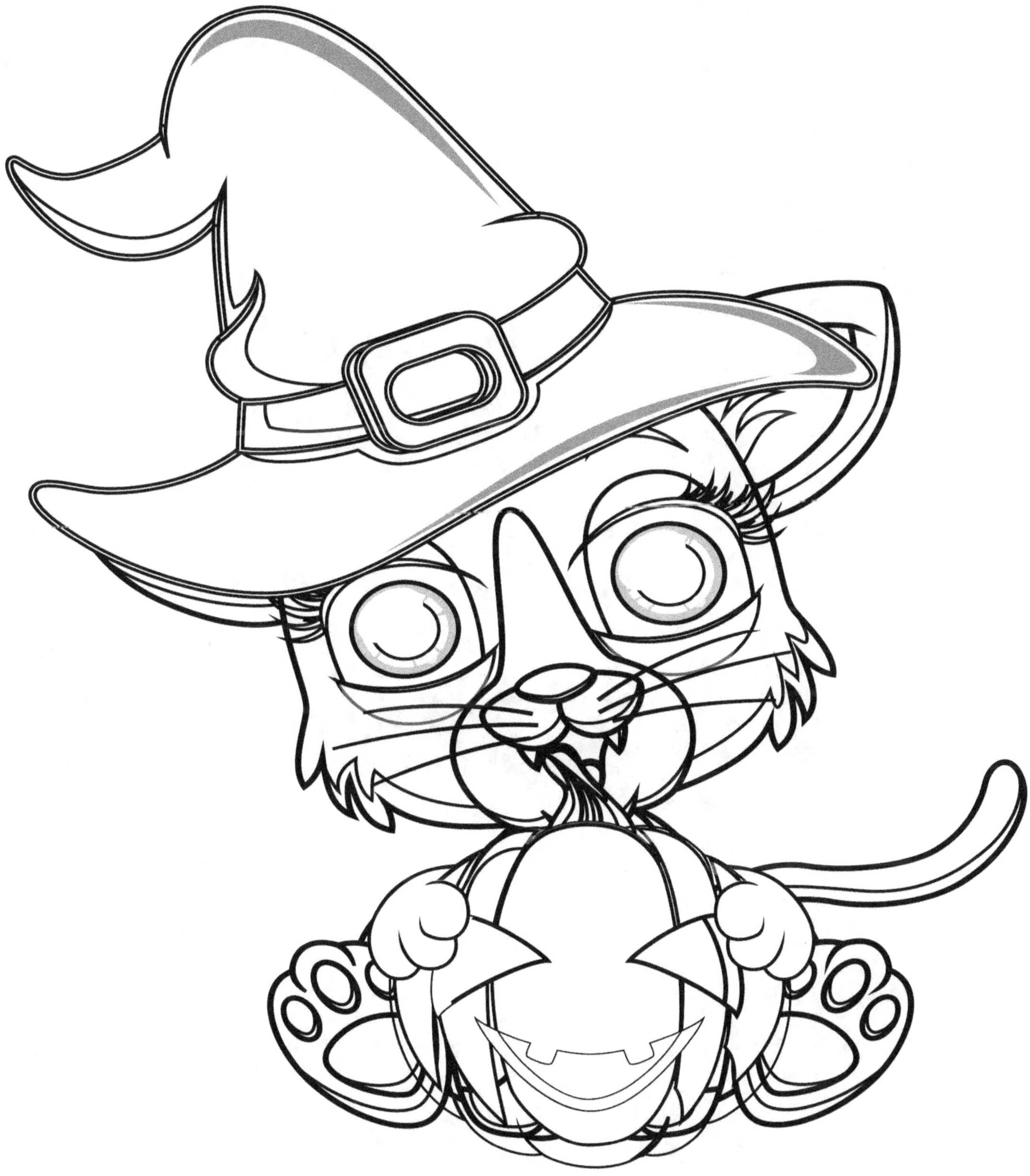

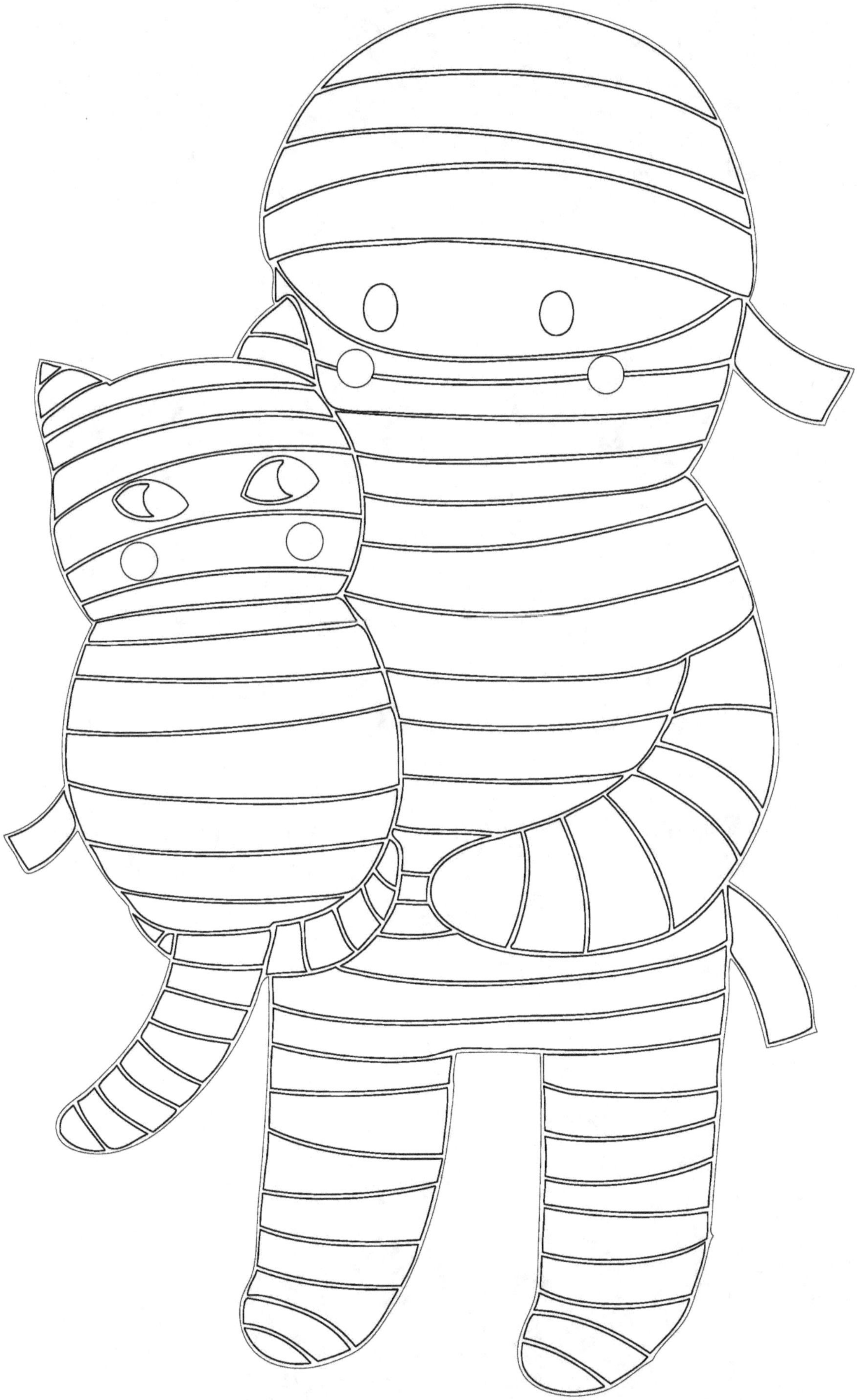

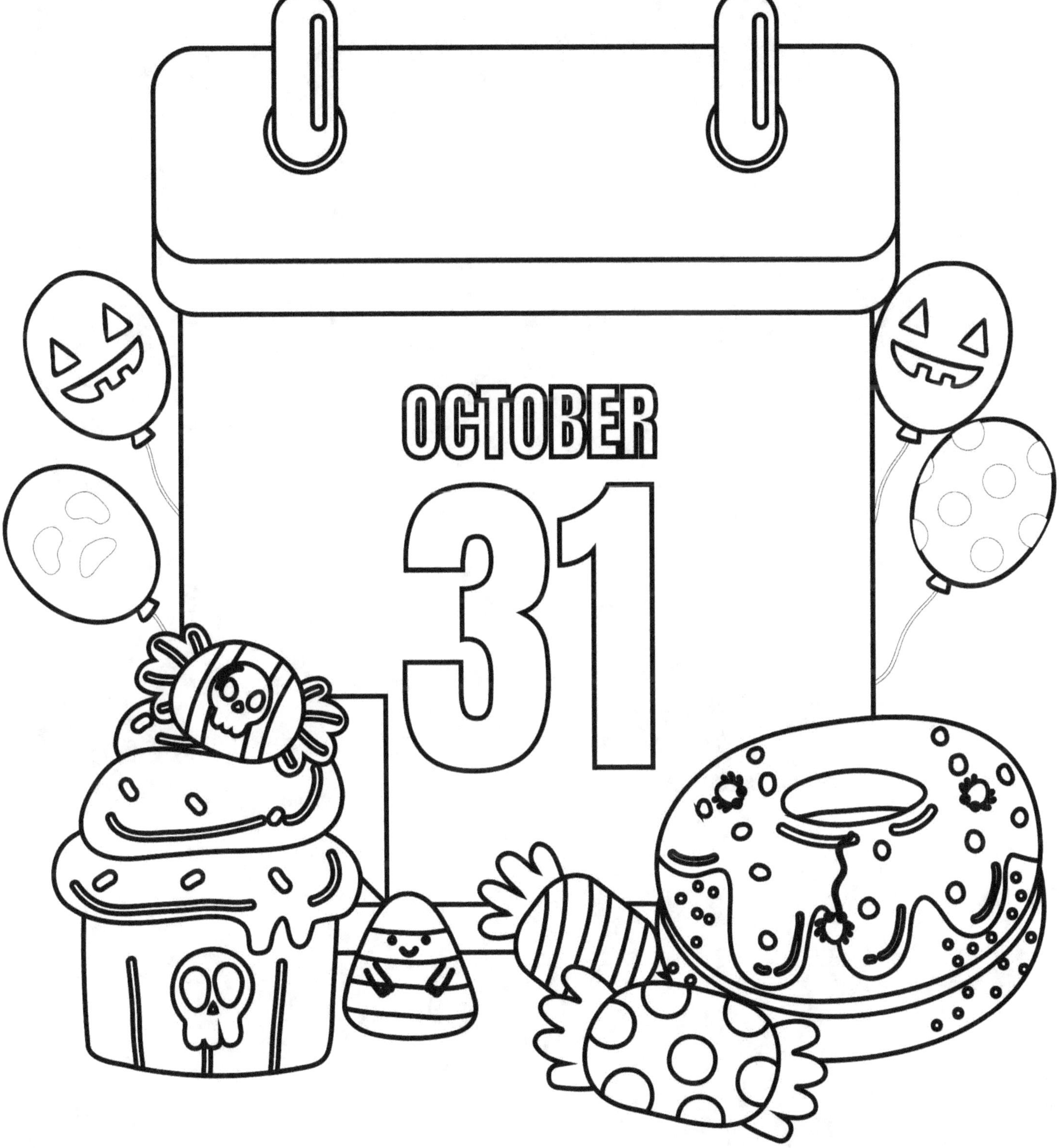
OCTOBER
31

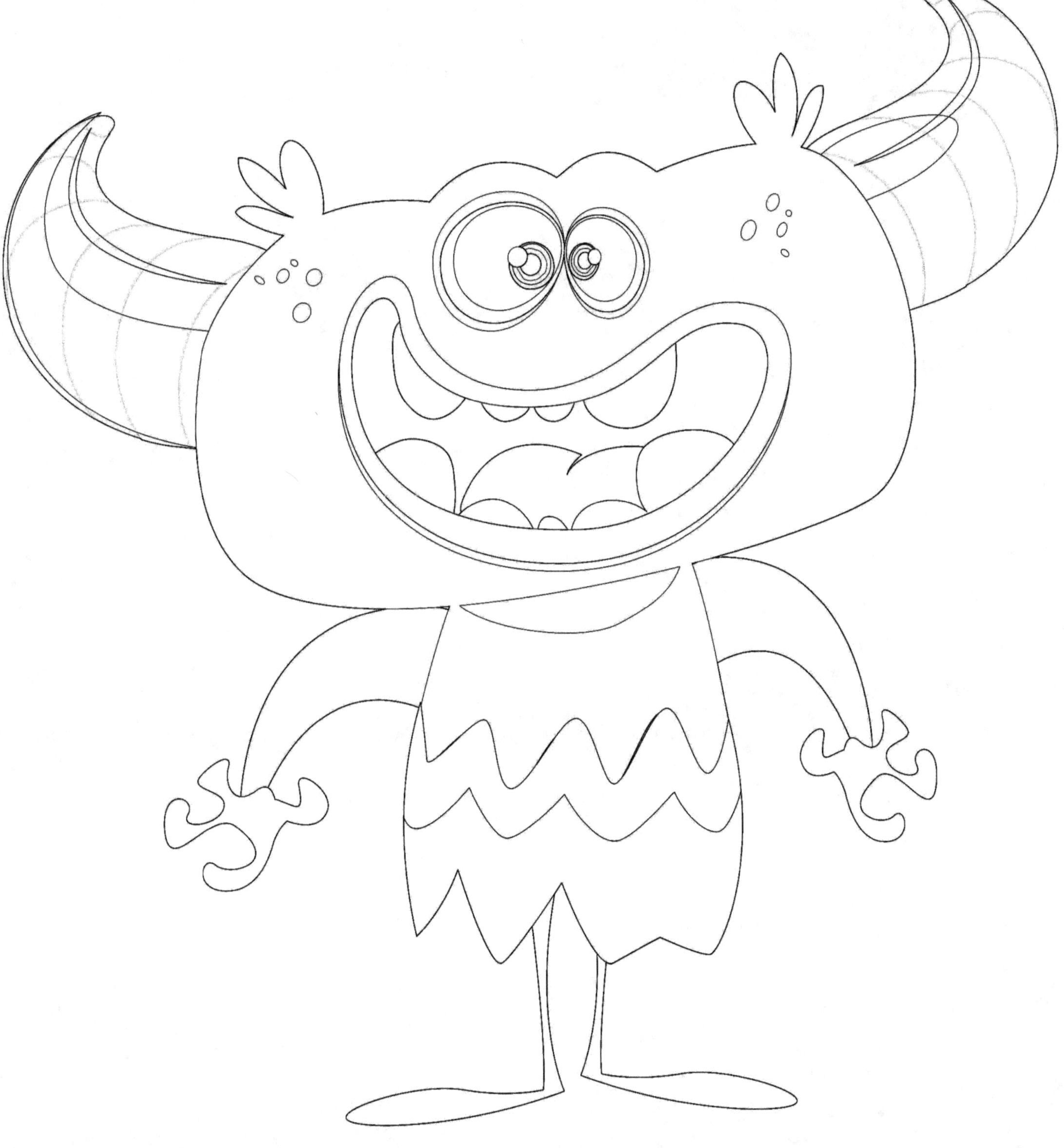

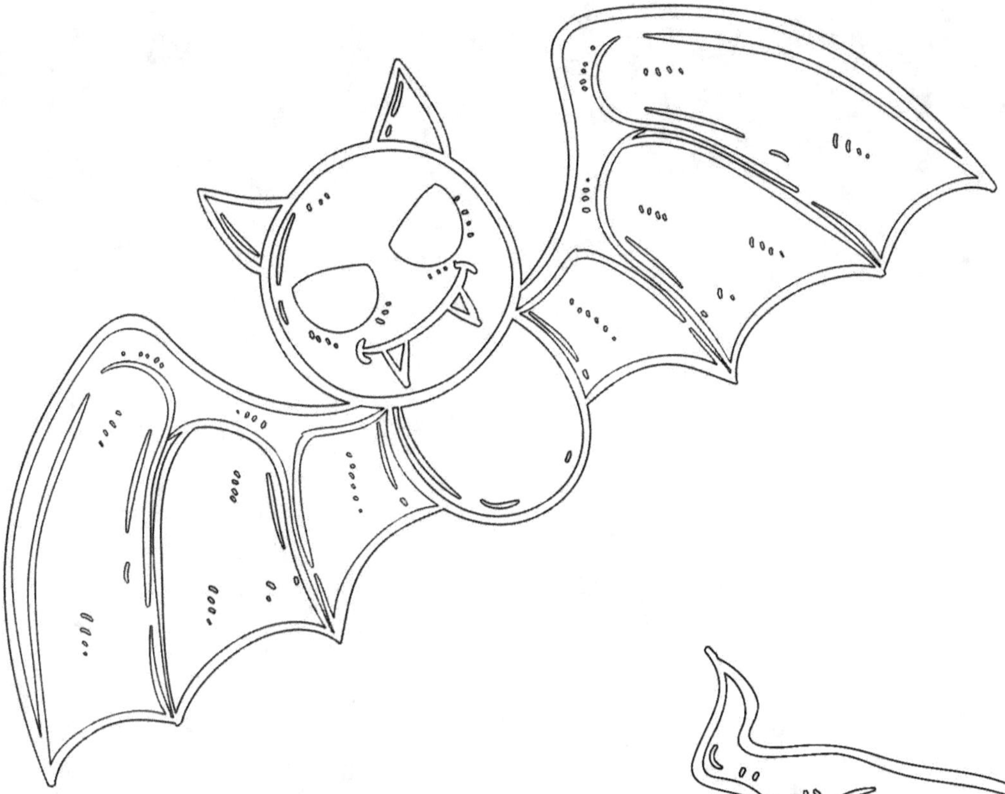
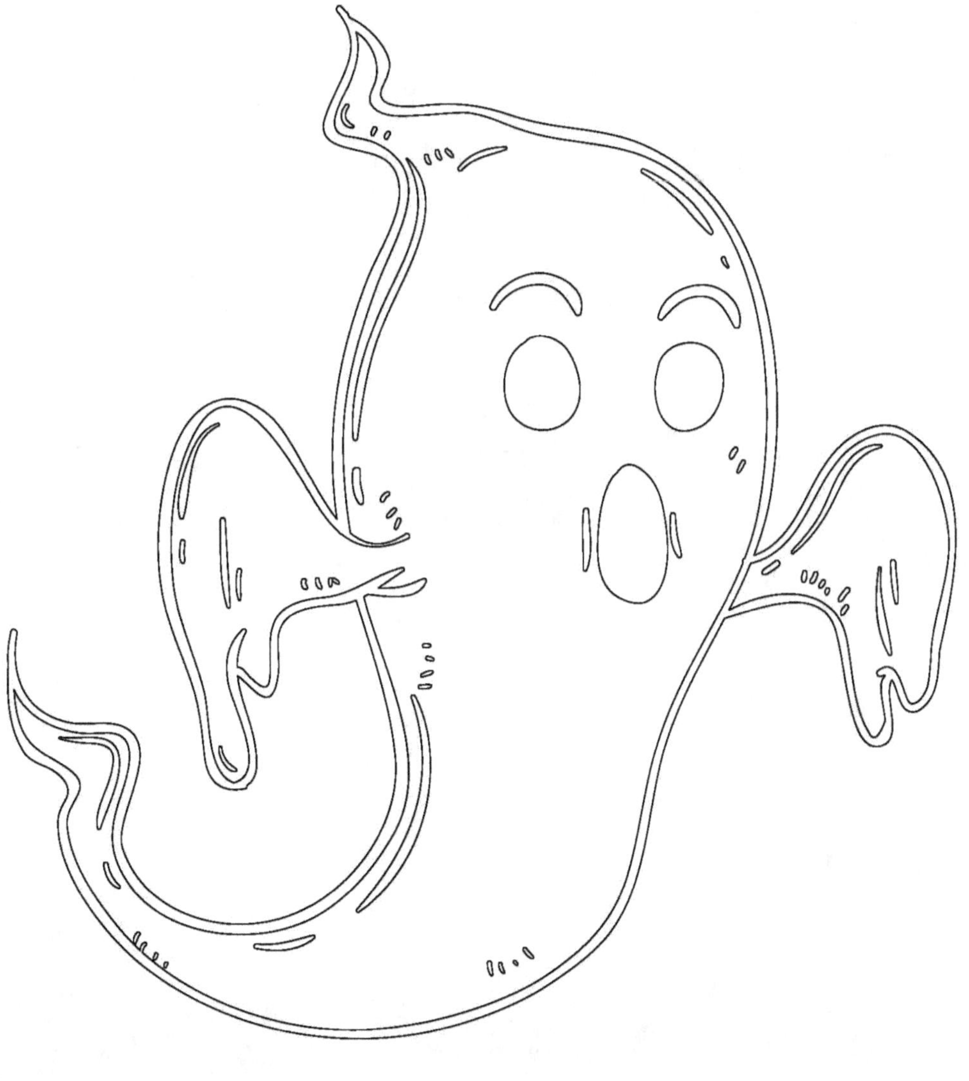

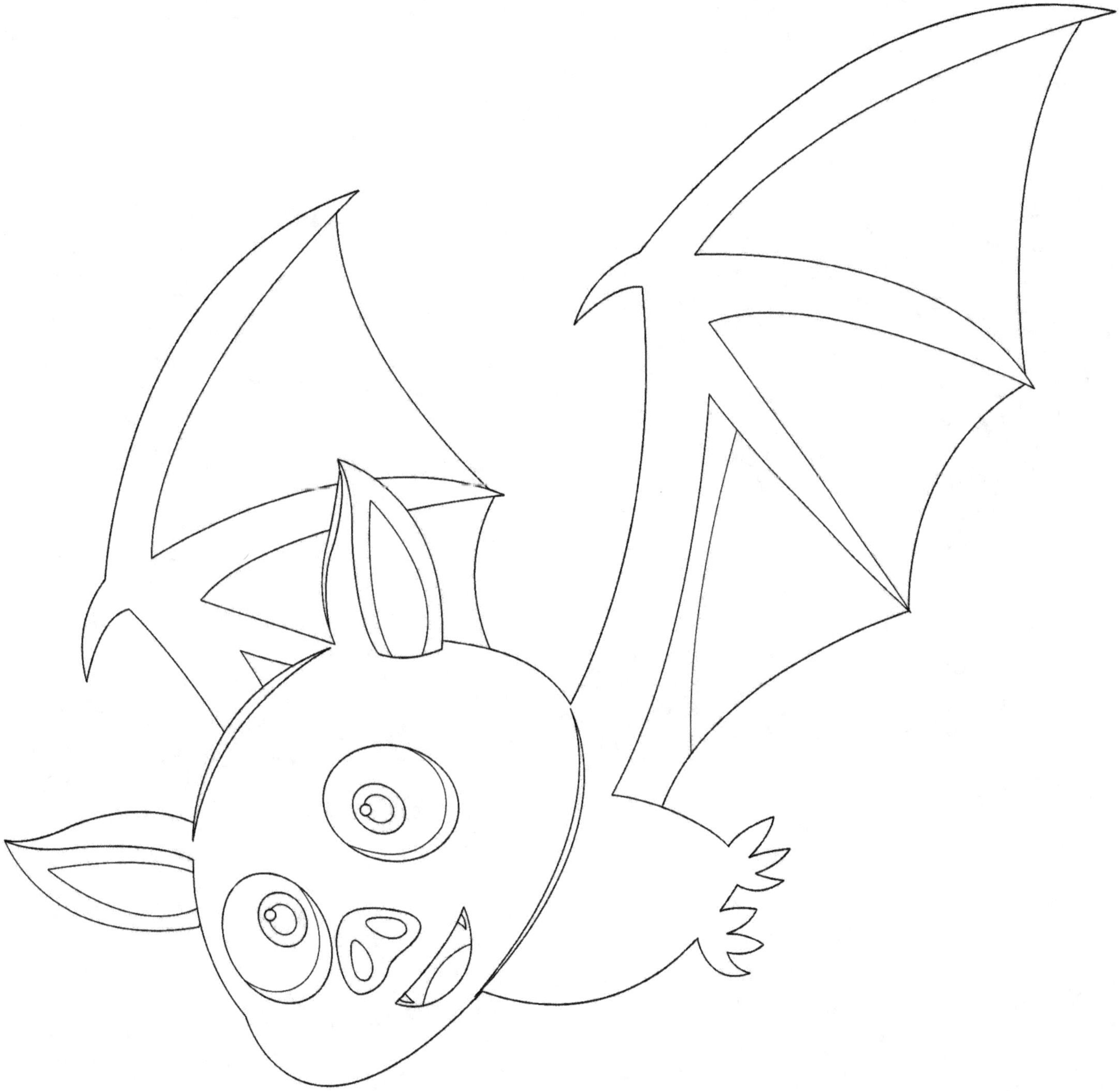

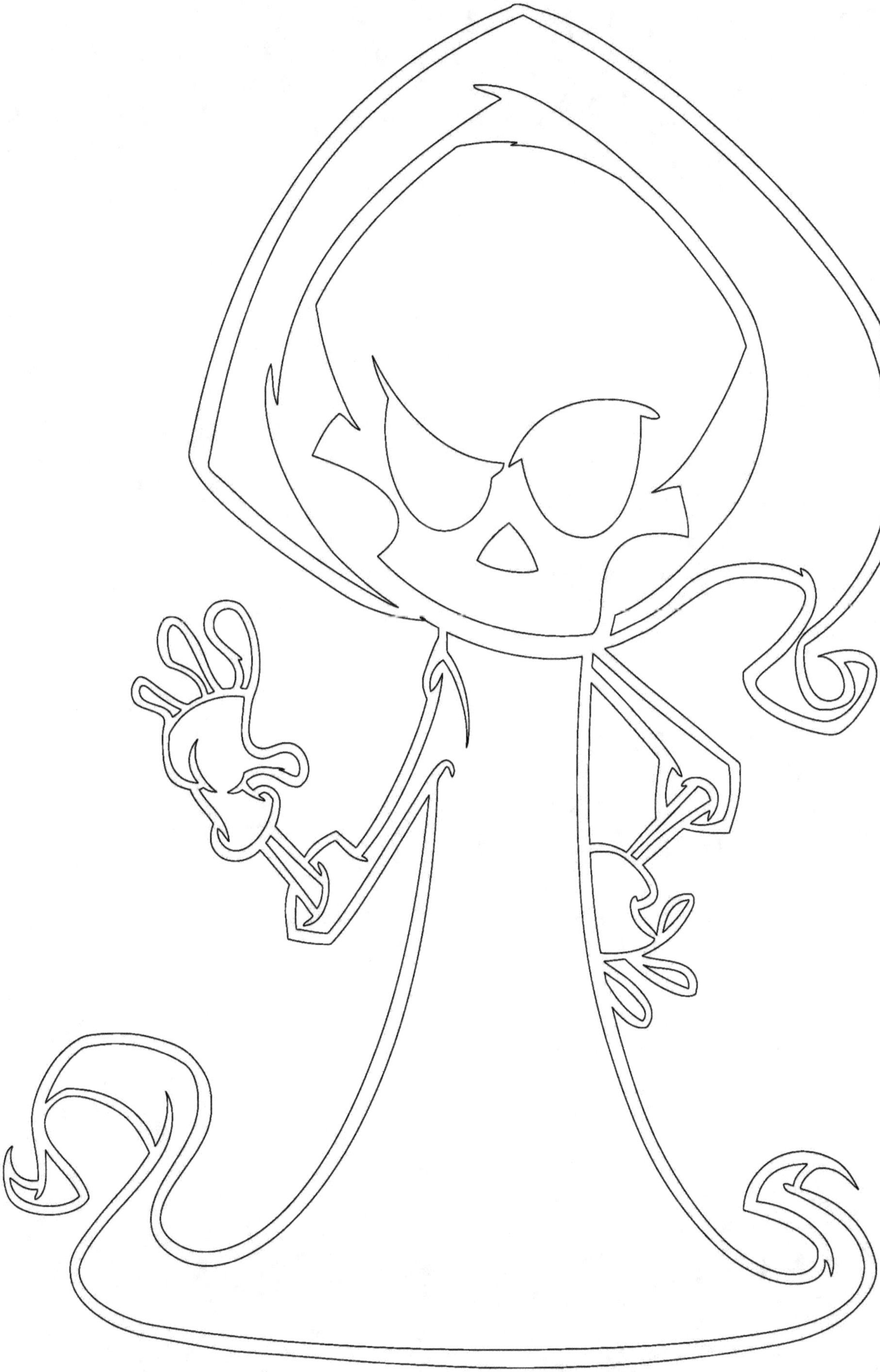

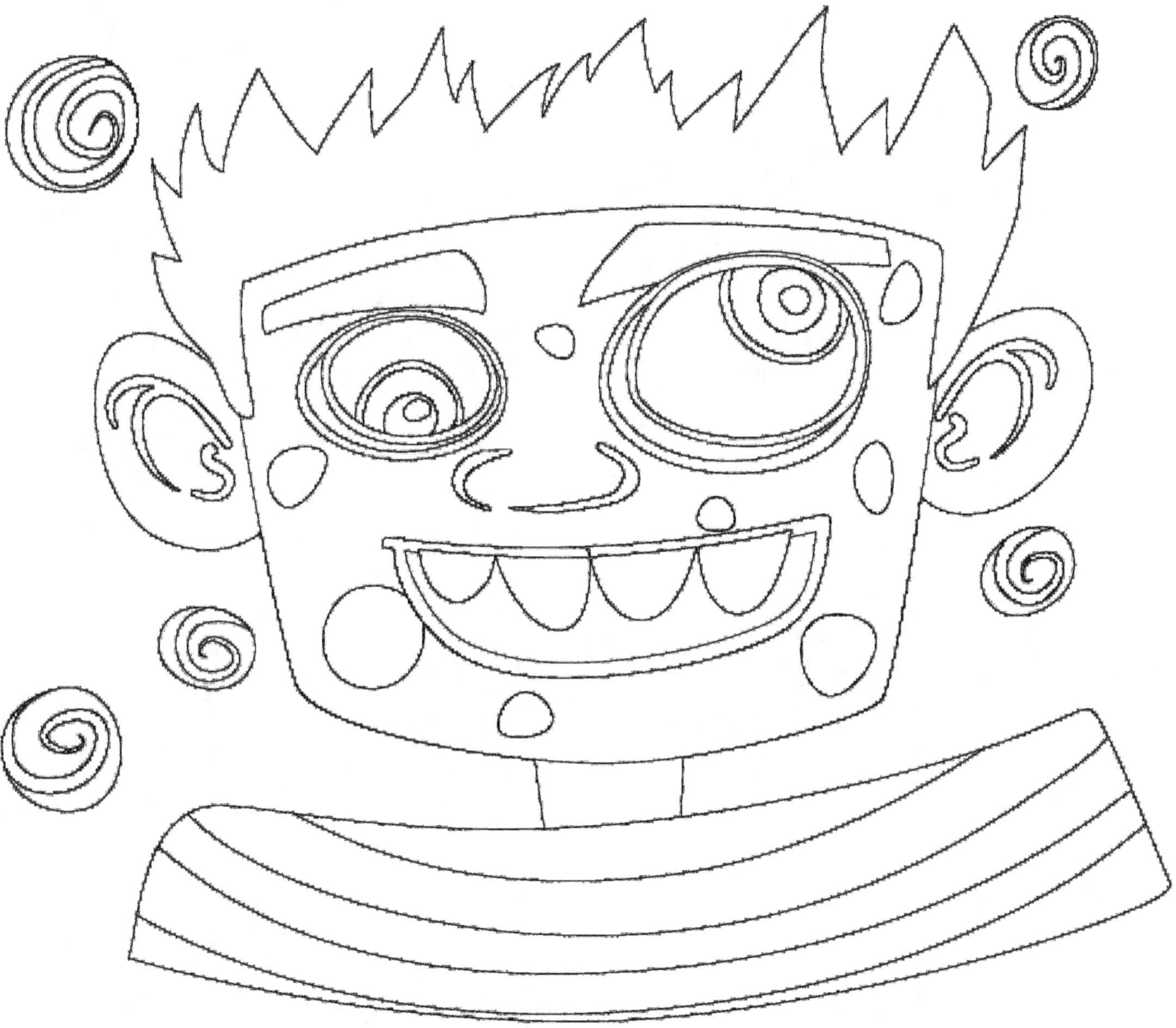

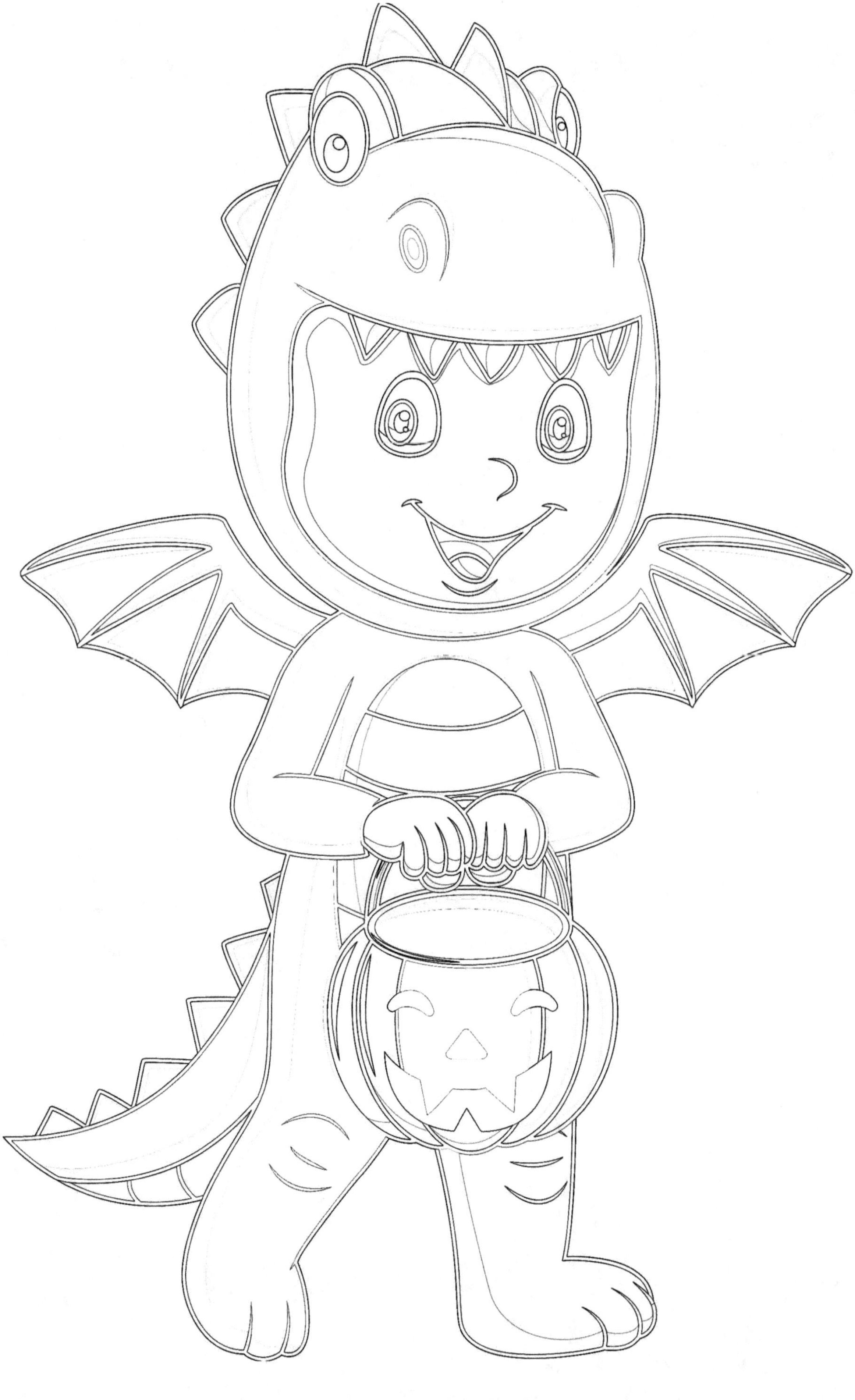

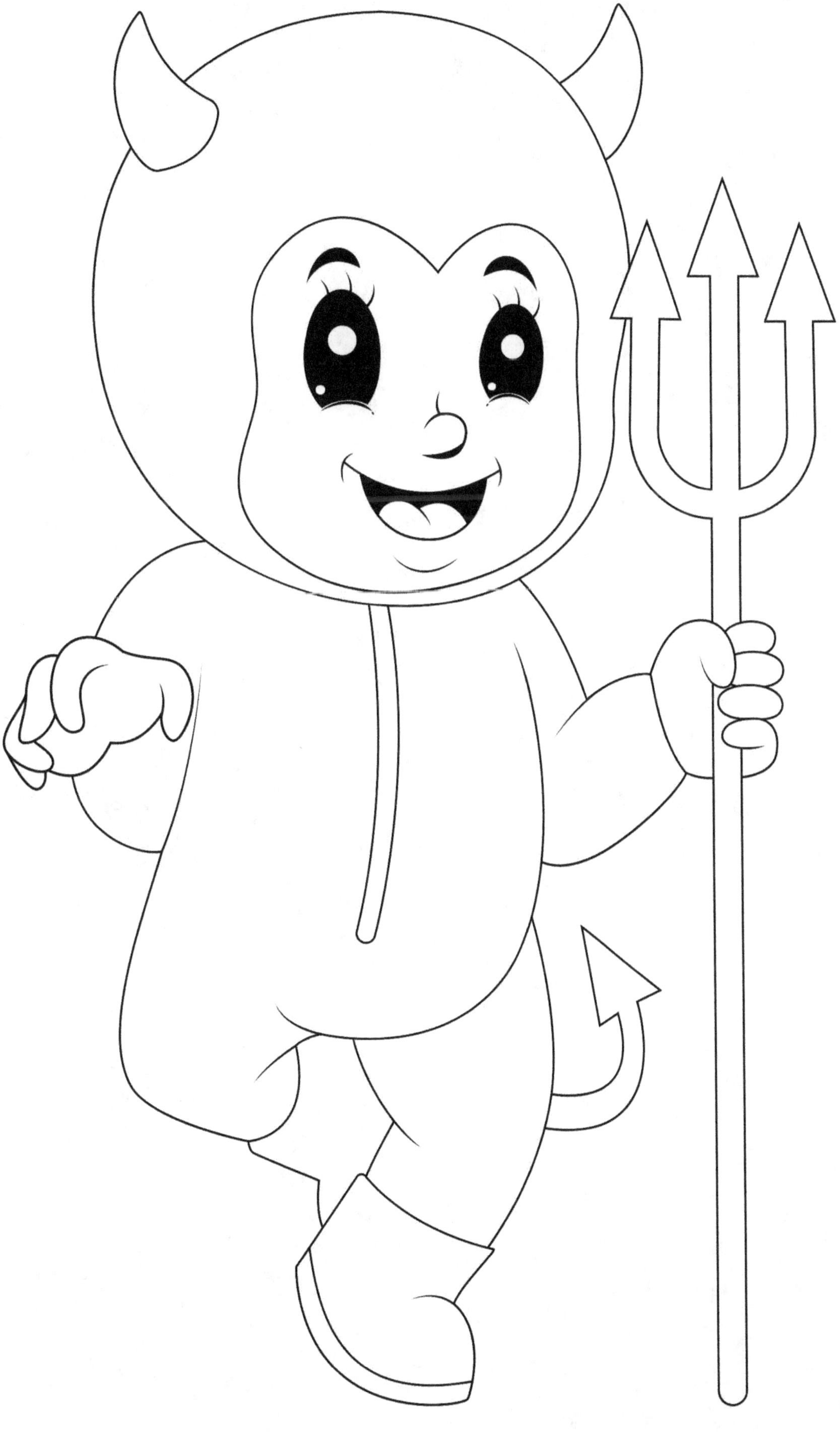

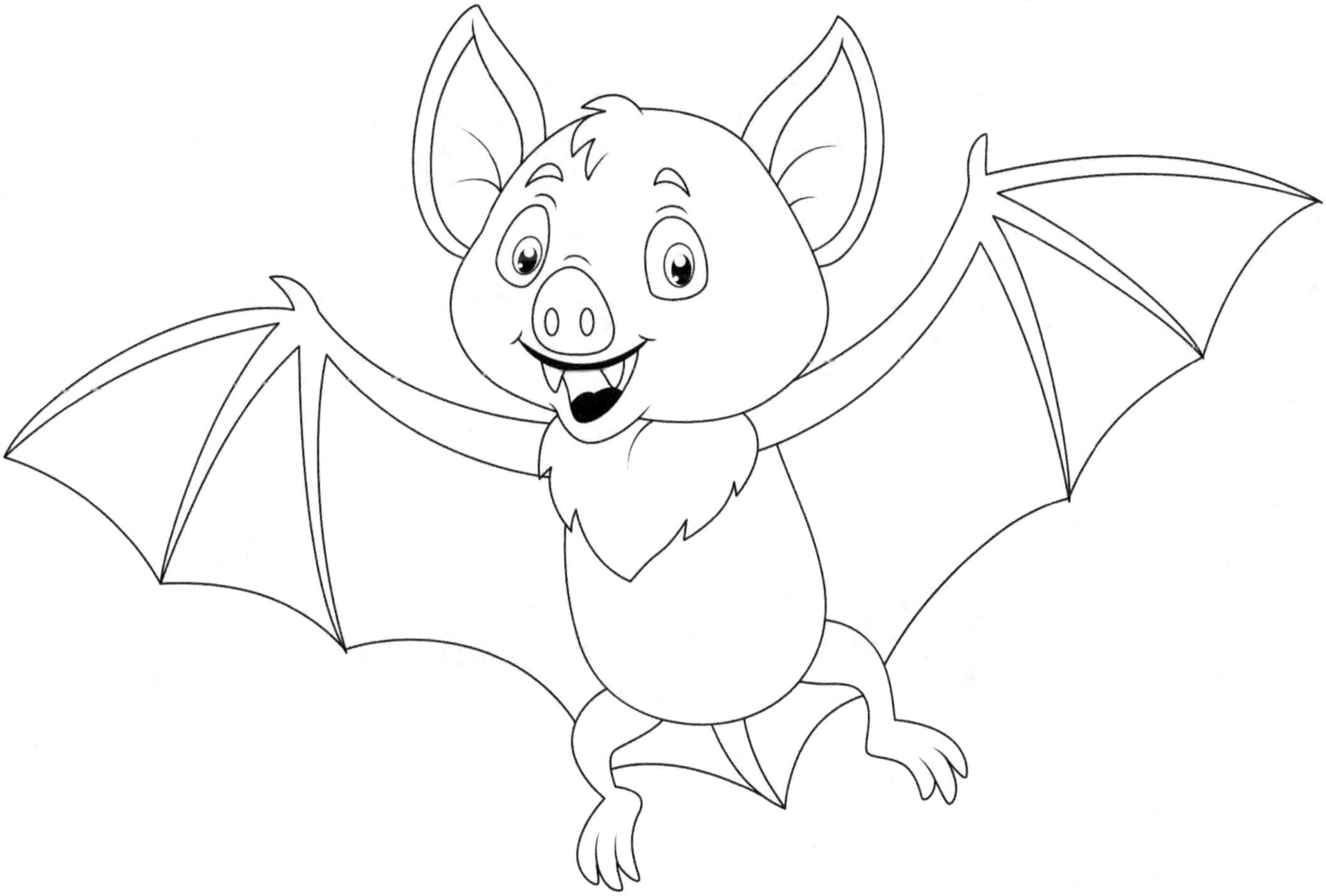

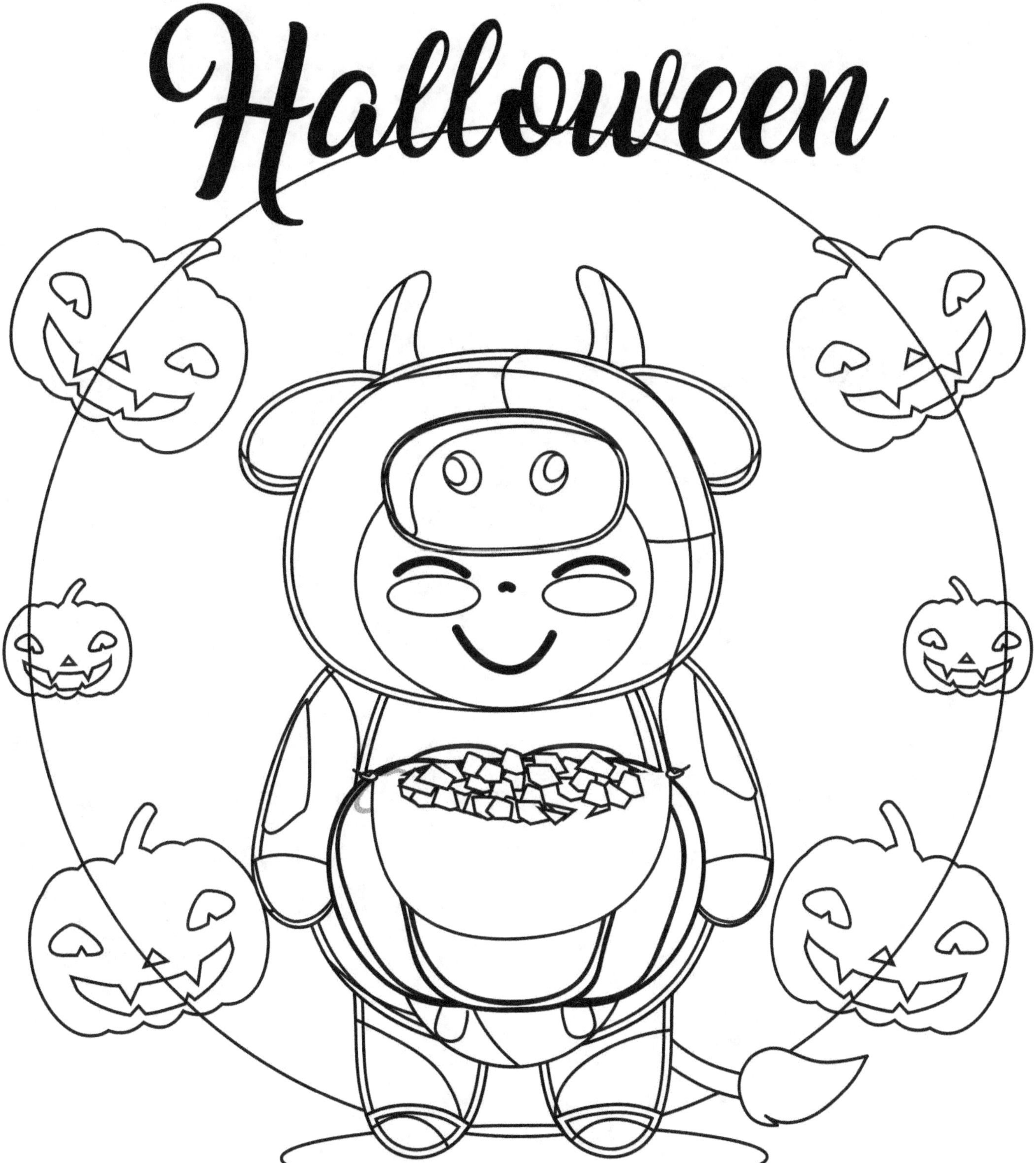
Halloween

www.ingramcontent.com/pod-product-compliance
Lightning Source LLC
Chambersburg PA
CBHW080601220526
45466CB00010B/3211
* 9 7 8 1 7 0 0 1 4 6 5 5 7 *